"I laughed, my dog howled."

—Steve Martin

"Hy Conrad and Jeff Johnson must have been dogs in another life. Their wry and witty insights into the minds of dogs are downright uncanny. *Things Your Dog Doesn't Want You to Know* is hilarious and sensational."

—Rory Freedman, author of *Skinny Bitch*

"This is the perfect book for anyone who owns a dog, has ever owned one, or knows what a dog is. These guys made me laugh out loud—and captured my heart at the same time. The book is simply irresistible."

—Tony Shalhoub, star of the TV series *Monk*

"If everyone owned a dog, we would have world peace. If everyone reads this book, they will go and get a dog and we will have taken a big step in the right direction. So this book can save the world. It will definitely change your life."

—Terrence McNally, playwright

THINGS YOUR DOG
Doesn't Want
YOU TO KNOW

11 COURAGEOUS CANINES **TELL ALL**

HY CONRAD + JEFF JOHNSON

ART DIRECTION BY DEAN STEFANIDES

 sourcebooks

Photo credits for *Things Your Dog Doesn't Want You To Know*
Page 1: Gabby: Ryan KC Wong/iStockphoto; Dimples: Jovanka Novakovic/iStockphoto; Rufus T: Erik Lam/iStockphoto; Orson: Al Braunworth/iStockphoto; Moonbeam: Martine Roch/Gettyimages; Sophie: Fanelie Rosier/iStockphoto; Tinkerbell: Chris Collins; Sarge: Nick Measures/iStockphoto; Axelrod: Ivan Pavlisko/iStockphoto; Page 2, refrigerator background: Fabinus08/Dreamstime.com; Page 3, ham/page 29, fish/page 67, sausage/page 127, burger/page 182, turkey/page 183, steak/page 191, ribs: lumpynoodles/iStockphoto; Page 4, grassy/sky background: Embe2006/Dreamstime.com; Page 7, Tinkerbell with cake: Teresa Guerrero/iStockphoto; Page 8, clipboard background: Roberto1977/Dreamstime.com; Page 10, wood background: Chubbywubby/Dreamstime.com; paisley: Irmairma/Dreamstime.com; binder clips: Summersky/Dreamstime.com; Page 14, corkboard background: Sofia Kravchenko/Dreamstime.com; push pins/paper: Ika767/Dreamstime.com; Page 18, safety pins: Nadezda Razvodovska/Dreamstime.com; Page 19, director's chair: hero30/iStockphoto; Page 20, chalkboard background: Madmaxer/Dreamstime.com; Page 23, black photo corners: Samantha Grandy/iStockphoto; Page 25, woman kissing dog: Lapointe/iStockphoto.com; Page 31, puppy: Vladimir Suponev/iStockphoto; Page 37, dog chewing bone: AntiGerasim/iStockphoto; Page 39, leash/page 179, dirt: Lisa Thornberg/iStockphoto; Page 53, cheesecake/page 91, cake/page 115, donut, cookies, sundae/page 143, sundae/page 217, ice cream sandwich: Oksana Pravdina/iStockphoto; Page 54–55, hands: lightmax/iStockphoto; Page 59, laying boxer: Lise Gagne/iStockphoto; Page 64, tail: Tatiana Rodionova/iStockphoto; Page 1: Bandana/Page 65, tail (top)/page 169, skunk, pages 174–175, duck/page 187, growling Chihuahua: Eric Isselee/iStockphoto; page 65, tail (middle): Mark Hayes/iStockphoto; tail (bottom): Dusan Kostic/iStockphoto; Page 72–73, mushrooms: Floortje/iStockphoto; Page 79, mailman: Steve Snyder/iStockphoto; Page 89, sleeping dog (top): Katherine Moffitt/iStockphoto; sleeping dog (middle): Jeff Nagy/iStockphoto; sleeping dog (bottom): reesee_tereesee/iStockphoto; Page 103, sleeping puppies: DenGuy/iStockphoto.com; Page 109, Chihuahua in raincoat Teresa Guerrero/iStockphoto; Page 111, puppies: Jennifer Byron/iStockphoto; Page 120, fire hydrant: pagadesign/iStockphoto; Page 121, tree: kertlis/iStockphoto; Page 127, dog in wedding dress: Miranda Gerlock; Page 133, growling dog (top left): zilli/iStockphoto; growling dog (top right): Natallia Yaumenenka/iStockphoto; growling dog (bottom): Sarah Salmela/iStockphoto; Page 144–145, dog biscuits/page 167, dog biscuits: Tina Rencelj/iStockphoto; Page 153, digging dog: Erna Vader/iStockphoto; Page 159, sleeping dog: Rachel Jean/iStockphoto; Page 177, possum: Classix/iStockphoto; Pages 196–197, fleas: Armando Frazao/iStockphoto; Page 201, blue ribbon: Michael Krinke/iStockphoto; Page 203, jumping dog (top), jumping bog (bottom): Mark Coffey/iStockphoto; Page 207, woman: TommL/iStockphoto; Page 1, Charlie/Page 211, Schnauzers: Jen Grantham/iStockphoto; Page 223, laying dog: Deborah Cheramie/iStockphoto

Published by Sourcebooks, Inc.
P.O. Box 4410, Naperville, Illinois 60567–4410
(630) 961–3900
Fax: (630) 961–2168
www.sourcebooks.com

Library of Congress Cataloging-in-Publication Data

Conrad, Hy.
  Things your dog doesn't want you to know : 11courageous canines tell all / Hy Conrad and Jeff Johnson ; art direction, Dean Stefanides.
    p. cm.
  (pbk. : alk. paper) 1. Dogs—Miscellanea. 2. Dog owners—Miscellanea. 3. Dogs—Humor. 4. Dog owners—Humor. I. Johnson, Jeff, 1951- II. Title.
  SF426.2.C664 2012
  636.7—dc23

2011035365

Printed and bound in the United States of America.
VP 10 9 8 7 6 5 4 3 2 1

ACKNOWLEDGMENTS

We would like to thank our agent, Alice Martell, who thought this book was hilarious even before we wrote it. And Shana Drehs, who immediately "got it" and fought for us every step of the way. But most importantly, Hy and Jeff want to thank Dean Stefanides for his talent and skill in finding a visual "voice" for each dog. Thanks to him, people don't even have to read the book in order to enjoy it.

DEDICATION

To the Florida Keys SPCA and
open door shelters everywhere.

FROM THE EDITORS

For centuries, dogs have kept their secrets to themselves, refusing to share them even with their best human friends. There are many reasons for this. First, dogs are typically shy. And humans don't always ask the right questions. Both species have a natural desire to maintain privacy. And last but not least, dogs can't talk.

At least, that's what we thought. But with persistence and patience and half a ton of treats, we have managed to convince eleven dogs from all walkies of life to come forward. This is finally their chance to tell us the things that other dogs can't—or won't: their hopes and dreams, their grudges and pleasures, and what they really think about you.

The following are their brave and revealing stories.

THE DOGS

Axelrod

YELLOW LAB

Lives in the suburbs with his family and a yard with an impossibly high fence. Graduated first in his private obedience class three times.

BANDANA

BORDER COLLIE

Bossy, with opinions about everything. He runs the household. It couldn't go on without him.

Dimples

BOXER

Recently gave birth to Mutt Junior and Runt, who are both still living at home. Disagrees with humans about parenting.

Tinkerbell

CHIHUAHUA

Lives in a mansion with the alpha human Margo and her equally human daughter Brianna. Can shed but prefers not to.

Orson

BULLDOG

A foodie. Has two working mommies who reluctantly indulge his obsession. Lives in a small apartment, which seems to be getting smaller.

Sophie
COCKER SPANIEL
Mother of 18. Grandmother of 168.
Great-grandmother of...? Living out her twilight
years with her original humans—and a cat.

SARGE
GERMAN SHEPHERD
A working dog who has spent his life going from one
dead-end job to another. Will work for scraps.

Charlie
MINIATURE SCHNAUZER
Found on the street with no memory of his past.
Adopted by a shelter employee. Lives with six other
dogs and considers his current situation foster care.

Moonbeam
MIXED BREED
Found stranded on a roof after a flood. Adopted by a
New Age follower. Hates her name.

Gabby
LONG-HAIRED DACHSHUND
Girlie and smart. She's at that awkward age
when she's just starting to notice boys.

Rufus T.
BLOODHOUND
A country dog who feels a little out of place.
His best friend is Toby, a boy he's known
almost from birth.

I WILL NEVER BE FULL

Looks like I'm starving, right? I stick my nose in the bowl a hundred times a day like the food is going to magically appear. I can beg while asleep. I pay attention to everything you two do in the kitchen, like you're some kind of master chefs, which you are not.

But you want to know the truth...? I haven't really been hungry since I was a week old and the other kids pushed me away from Mom. Ever since, I've just been in various stages of not-quite-full.

It's not like I'm obsessed. I do think about other things. Like taking a walk by the overflowing garbage cans that look so tasty and...I'm sorry, where was I? Oh yeah. I want to eat and eat until the fat on my cheeks blocks my eyes, until my skin expands and I explode like a brown and white balloon. Then I'll be happy.

Maybe it comes from back in the old-timey days when we were all wild beasts, starving without a scrap, until, whoa...there's this big kill, you know? And we all get to gorge ourselves on some kind of mastodon leg, fighting off everyone else, 'cause we know we're going to be starving again. Except that now the mastodon leg is a tofu burger hanging off that hibachi grill on your little balcony. And the starvation period was maybe five minutes.

By the way, sorry about the tofu. I was wrong and it wasn't very good. But it was yours, not mine, and I totally get the need for boundaries. Um...where was I?

I probably shouldn't mention this either, but ever since you two have been mad and not talking to each other, I'm getting two dinners at night. But did I give you any indication that she just gave me a full bowl of kibble? Like, just two minutes ago? Was I any less enthusiastic? Did I turn up my nose and say, "No thanks, I just ate. Why don't I save this for tomorrow?" No, that would have been rude.

And dogs aren't rude. Cats are.

Orson

I Like the Herb Garden

We're not that different, me and you. We both like long walks on the leash, taking up the entire bed at night. And that thing you do with the ball, pretending to throw it and making it disappear? Love that. Can't get enough.

So it shouldn't be a surprise that I like a smelly bathroom. I remember as clear as yesterday—maybe it was yesterday. I was taking a drink from the downstairs toilet when I noticed how weird it smelled. All flowery and herby.

It took me barely an hour to figure out it was coming from that little dish beside the wrapped-up soap. There were all sorts of leaves and buds and petals. Yum. It tasted even better than the soap. A bit dry. But nothing a sip of blue water couldn't fix.

After that, my breath smelled great, until I ate the rabbit droppings. Then it smelled better. But it got me thinking how humans must like this particular smell, the mix of pee and those herby flowers. And let me just say, if you guys like it, I like it. I live to like what you like.

For a while I tried peeing down the side of the toilet, like you do sometimes at night. But then the bathroom door started to be shut all the time and I couldn't get in anymore, no matter how hard I scratched.

Anyway, did you know there were all these smelly plants in the garden by the side of the kitchen? You must know, 'cause I've seen you cut them off with scissors. And I thought, "Hey, if it's good enough for their bathroom, it's good enough for mine."

Thor from next door says this patch of ground is called an herb garden, just like the one in your bathroom. I've been peeing on it three or four times a day, mostly on the leafy things you put in your salads. I hope that's okay.

AXELROD

5

My Pack

 Willow

 NuNu

 Flea

Bit

Tinkerbell

You Can Forget My Birthday
By Tinkerbell

First off, I don't know when I was born. Honestly. My eyes were closed and I had no idea if I was still in or out, except that at one point it stopped being crowded. So I missed my original birthday, which I don't think is all that unusual.

Also, I'm not sure exactly when a year has gone by—or seven years as you like to put it. "Hey, everyone. Tink is, like, twenty-eight. Like, middle-aged. That's funny." Well, I'm not twenty-eight. I'm a vibrant four-year-old. But that's not my point entirely.

My point is we don't celebrate birthdays. If you really want to know, we celebrate naps and escaping from the backyard and the death of cats. Remember that time I altered the leather on your favorite shoes and you locked me in the closet and I altered the straps on your second-favorite shoes? That wasn't because you forgot my birthday the day before. No. They were just ugly. I was doing you a favor.

Also, I couldn't resist the irony of you punishing me for the first shoe crime by locking me in your shoe closet. That's why I ate the second pair, even though I wasn't in the mood.

So, about yesterday's party…I guess I liked the attention and all my friends coming over.

But it wasn't much different from a hundred other playdates, except maybe for the tent in the backyard and the doggie cupcakes with the lighted candles. And later on, of course, the fire truck and the water hoses.

But all that other stuff—before the flaming tent and the water…oh, and before the bleeding, screaming clown—some of that early stuff was lame. Like making us do karaoke. And hair extensions. They just don't look natural on me.

Oh, about the clown incident. The dogs had this bet going about whether that was his real nose. And whether those were his real shoes. And, tell me, really, what kind of clown shows up wearing his own nose and shoes? I mean, losing a bet like that is enough to drive you rabid. Anyway…

Next year.

Tails up

I HAVE THIS HABIT

Back when I was a few months old, I got my first taste of the stuff. From that moment on, I guess I was hooked. But it's not my fault. Let me tell you my side.

It all started on the playground. Officer Simon was this police guy who used to hang out at the Obedience Academy where me and my brothers went to school. I remember how he picked me out from the others. "That's the one," he seemed to be saying. Then he took me away and pressed a bean bag right in my face. "Smell it. Smell the pot. Get a good whiff." At the time, I had no idea that it was just some cheap Simi Valley shwag. I just knew it smelled fantastic.

Seconds later, my new friend Simon hid that bean bag somewhere on the playground and told me to go find it. "You want the stash, boy? Yes, you want it. Go find the stash." This time I took a good bite before he could grab it back from me. Wow. We did it a dozen more times that day, until I started drooling and barking at anything, even if it wasn't funny or important.

From what I hear, my story's not unusual. The first few times, you're a good boy and they give you the stuff for free. Then you get hooked and they make you start working for it.

Now I spend most of my time dozing and licking myself and trying to remember where the water bowl is. Officer Simon and I go out a few times a week, visiting farms and parts of downtown that have a whole lot of smells. When I find a stash of pot, I always try to eat a little before I jump and bark and signal a bust. Sometimes I even hide a little under my collar. For later.

Some of my fellow drug dogs call my kind of behavior dangerous. They say pot is a gateway drug, but I don't believe it. Sometimes I do find it by a gateway, yes. But more often than not it's under a futon or on a shelf beside an X-Box.

Oh, and there's talk now of training me to track down cocaine, or maybe heroin. Because I'm so good.

SARGE

Your Psychic Is a Fake

I'm grateful, don't get me wrong. I'm not just some dumb mutt who went through a flood and doesn't know how lucky she is. I'm lucky. And smarter than most. Take, for example, that thing you hang over my bed. You call that a dream catcher and you think it'll take away all the bad dreams from the flood, even though it's just feathers and string. A bunch of useless feathers and string. Like I said, smarter than most.

But you can't help worrying about me. You watch me guard my bowl when I eat and you wonder what horrible thing made me so nervous, instead of just thinking, "This is one clever dog who knows how to protect her food from unseen danger, like a pack of hungry cats."

When I started acting more weird, you took me to the vet. Then to a dog psychiatrist. And when no one could figure out what was wrong, we drove over to your psychic who also is a pet psychic. Sure, why not?

The psychic is a nice enough lady with a soft voice. Her place smelled even more like incense than yours, but without the dog urine to tone it down. As soon as we got there, she laid her eight scratchy rings and the fingers inside them on my head and made a lot of moans. I moaned back. It seemed polite.

You told her about my weird problem: how I go out in the yard during the full moon and just sit there and howl and howl. For hours. I never do it any other night, like when it's almost full or the day after it's full. Only on the full moon. Even when there are clouds and you can't really see the moon.

It didn't take long for her to read my mind. According to her, I'm not upset by the moon but by the gravitational force and the atmospheric pressure. These conditions, she says, are exactly like they were back home on the night before the flood. And the howling is just my way of trying to warn you that another flood is coming. It all made sense. I was impressed.

Of course, there's another possible explanation. Go ask your next-door neighbor.

It seems that he likes incense and dream catchers as much as you. He also goes into his backyard and lies naked on the grass during the full moon and blows on a high-pitched dog whistle for hours on end, which I find very annoying.

I think he likes to hear me howl.

☮ Moonbeam

You're Spoiling My Kids

I think I'm a good mother. You must think so too, because this time you let me keep two of them, which is better than a lot of single mothers in my situation. The boys are certainly a mouthful. Runt still sticks by my side as much as possible, while his brother, Mutt Junior, is pretty rambunctious.

I like having them here, and I don't want to quibble. But it seems you took over the mothering job from me, except for the milk part (I am so glad that's over). And if you don't mind my saying so, you're spoiling them.

This is not the same way you raised me. First, there's no crate. Call me old-fashioned, but I think every child needs a crate. Just having a little gate across the kitchen door is pitiful. And a crate would help prepare them for some important things later in life. Like kennels.

Next is this business of chewing furniture. I remember you being very strict with me. I must have still been on my first sofa leg when you scolded me and stuffed me back in the crate. By leg number six, I learned.

Now, I see Junior attacking the same legs of the very same sofas I ate. And all you do is smile in that helpless way, like you're thinking, "Dogs will be dogs." But that's not true. Dogs will still be puppies if you don't raise them.

Speaking of sofas, you used to worry so much about dog hair and keeping me in my place. Now Junior and Runt jump on anything they want. And don't even talk to me about house-training. I've never seen so much praise given out for something so normal. When Runt finally lifted his leg on a tree...you guys embarrassed yourselves.

Then there's the whole business of manners. What manners? Exactly. With me, you at least made the effort: shake hands when you're introduced; don't speak to the mailman through the door; the cheese is for guests. Now your first reaction is to giggle, grab the camera, and take a video.

There have to be rules, dear. I learned that early. I would see the disappointment in your eyes. "Maybe getting a dog was a mistake," you'd think. "Is it too late to take her back?" And I would try to do better. But now...

If you ask me, it's only going to lead to problems.

Dimples

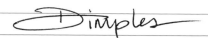

JUNiOR + RuNt = SPOiLeD RoTten

We were very excited when you first showed up. To tell the truth, days do get a little long. And even though we have dog doors and dog-houses and a whole big backyard, everyone can use an afternoon walk. We're just sorry that things got off to a rocky start. Maybe if I give you a few pointers...

First off, you can't walk all seven of us together. I think you learned that lesson. But it's also very important who you take with whom and when and where. It's simple.

Chloe has to be first, since she hates us and won't pee if we've been out there before her. But you can't walk her alone because that would upset Snowball, who gets jealous. I would recommend walking the girls together but keeping them twenty or thirty feet apart for safety. Except, of course, if it's sweltering hot (Snowball faints easily) or if one of them has a urinary tract infection. Then you should leave Snowball behind and walk Chloe with a male of a similar temper, usually me or Jake unless we're not in the mood to deal with Chloe.

Duke must be in the second group, or else he'll fall behind and bite at your heels. No one knows why. Jake can be in this group too, unless he's with Chloe in the first group. And Buster has to be with Jake, unless there are more than three dogs in this group, which I wouldn't recommend.

During the winter, Miley can be in group three, except if there's snow. Then she goes in a special group four, with snow booties. Duke is also in the snow booties group, although you have to make sure you have the right size, since he's old and his feet swell. But don't try booties on Buster. Buster's paranoid about his feet.

Group three also has the dogs who like to run. That can be me or Jake or Buster if we're not in a previous group. If Miley is here, then you have to carry her for part of the run since she's not much into exercise.

If rain is involved, you need to do exactly the opposite of the above advice. This is essential. Sleet rules are the same as snow rules plus rain rules but minus the booties rule. Very cold weather means jackets, but only for the girls, unless there's wind. Then everyone gets a jacket, except Buster, who still thinks you're too close to his feet. I hope this explains it.

I couldn't help but notice that you haven't been around for a few days. I assume this is just because of your injuries and has nothing to do with anything we might have accidentally said or done. Please hurry back.

Charlie

My Opinion of Boys

I suppose I always liked boys. Whenever I ran into one, it seemed like the most natural thing just to roll over on my back and lie there wagging my tail. Don't know why. Sometimes this felt a little subtle, so I also wriggled back and forth and whimpered. Just a bit. I didn't want to seem easy.

The story was always the same. A little wag and sniff then on to the next and—flop, right back down on my back. "Hi, there." No big deal.

Until last week. Then the boys changed. I swear I had nothing to do with it. But they all started wanting to do more. Even the shy ones who never gave me a second sniff. I had to fight them off. I mean, come on, guys. What part of lying on my back and whimpering don't you understand? I'm not in the mood. I even bit a few on the nose, I got so angry.

And then came today. How could I have been so stupid? Boys are phenomenal. They're sweet and caring and...did you notice how they smell? And not just one. I think they all must have rolled around on the same raccoon, because every single boy smells great, some kind of earthy...or maybe that's me. Could be. I don't know and I don't care.

This is probably why you decided to keep me inside. Ever since I scratched my way through that flimsy screen door and started running straight for the house with the big Irish family down the street. I just wanted to say hello, honest. And they just wanted to say hello to me. I could tell by the howling. Irish setters howl a lot, don't they?

I can't imagine feeling any different, and it's driving me crazy. So I think we should come to a compromise. You let me out to meet as many boys as I want. And at some point, I promise to come home. Okay? All the other girls are doing it, you know. At least the ones that live with that breeder we met. I know that for a fact.

UPDATE: Never mind. I don't know what got into me, but I'm over it. Wow. I gotta remember never to do this again.

♡ Gabby

The Things I'm Dreaming

This was a good day.

First I wake Toby up with a big slobbery lick and before you know it, me and him are out in the woods, the two of us pissing on trees like crazy. I like it when humans leave their scent outside. I can smell it for maybe a month, and it makes everywhere feel right at home.

Then we amble down the railroad tracks and over to the double-wide where my mamma still lives with a couple of my half brothers. A girl lives there who Toby likes. She comes outside and Toby shows off. He takes a ribbon from her hair and tells her to hide it somewhere in the junk pile. It takes me no time at all to find it and bring it back. It's a good trick. But then Toby forgets to give it back. Forgets on purpose. He puts the ribbon in his own pocket, and all the way home I smell the ribbon and I tease him by nudging it with my nose. We tease each other like that.

In the afternoon, Toby's family comes over. The men all go hunting with me. This is what I was trained for, chasing and treeing raccoons. We have a good time too, running through the crunchy leaves and gulping the crisp air. Afterward, they all say that I'm the best hound ever.

Later on, the men watch football, while the women cook in the kitchen and watch *Annie*, an old movie they must've seen a hundred times. Me, I lie down on the cool linoleum and ask everyone to step around me if they would, please.

At some point, I guess I must have fallen asleep. I do remember being just awake enough to know I was moving my legs and making little yelpy sounds. Everyone saw me and laughed. They thought I was running in my sleep. Dreaming about the hunt and looking so happy.

Actually, I was dreaming about *Annie*. And I wasn't running. I was dancing. And singing. It must be so wonderful and glamorous, don't you think? Being a dog in the movies, like Sandy, and getting to do all the big production numbers and being famous?

If I could, I would trade being a coon hound for being a movie star. Any day of the week. Anyway, that's what I was dreaming.

Rufus T.

FOLLOW MY LEAD

Let me make this simple. I'm in charge of the house—from getting people up every morning to announcing the mealtimes, even reminding you to put out fresh water for the dog. Do you really think you control the kind of friends your teenage kids bring into the house after school? Really? Guess again.

I'm not sure you realize how much I do. Take, for example, the stove. It's dangerous. I know because one day I smelled something good and I put my paws up there, just to get a sniff. Instead I got burned. Conclusion? Stoves are hot. Very often you forget this. Every day I see you getting much too close. I've even seen you taking paper towels and wiping the top of it. That's why I bark at you in the kitchen. Not a lot, maybe a half hour or until I give up.

Same thing with closing the door. Ever since I was young, you've been yelling at everyone about that. (I won't name names, but apparently someone still runs out into the street and chases cars.) But every now and then you or one of the kids forgets this simple rule, usually in the evening when I'm tired and pretending to sleep.

Just last night you were in the front yard talking to the neighbor family—with the door wide open. I had to drag myself off a pile of comfortable laundry and close the door with my own mouth. Then, just to make sure, I ran around the house, making sure all the other doors were closed too. I don't know how you got back in, but I think you learned a lesson.

Then there's the matter of the leash. Sometimes when we get to the park or the dog run, you let yourself off the leash and just roam around on your own. This is a little reckless, since one of us could easily jump a fence and start chasing cars. Sometimes I do that just to teach you not to get off the leash.

It's a lot of work, but I think I run a pretty tight house. Oh, and as for the friends I let your kids bring up to their rooms...I don't know about you, but I prefer the ones who sneak in the cigarettes and alcohol. They're cool.

Bandana

I Can Poop the Second I Start My Walk

I shouldn't be telling you. This is a closely guarded secret in the dog world, a secret so big it could change the world as we know it. A huge scoop. And yes, I am aware that "scoop" has two meanings.

When we started doing this walk thing, I was young. You brought along the tiny treats and I was a good girl and then we went home. And then one time I got distracted. Before I knew it, we'd gone around the block twice. What a discovery. I could actually control the length of the walk. In theory, we could go forever, maybe as long as Sherman's march. (Sherman is the basset hound down the block with hemorrhoids. He can be out there for hours.)

Those first long walks were magical. We would go and keep going and you would sweet-talk me like it was you who wanted the tiny treat, not me. Then I finally pooped and you got so excited, like I'd just sat and rolled over and played dead all at the same time.

As time went on, I got a little bolder. How long could I drag this walk thing out? Not forever, after all. At some point, you lose your patience and just take me back inside. Then a little while later, nature calls and I have to do the whole hiding-the-poop-under-the-table trick, which never works. I don't know why I even try.

So we came to this kind of compromise, the kind where you don't know it's a compromise and I try to time out just how long your patience is. I'll sniff around and squat a few times and keep walking. And you'll keep your eye on my rear end like it's some kind of wrapped-up birthday present.

Now that I'm getting up there in dog years, the game isn't quite as much fun. The acting isn't really acting anymore. It does take me awhile to get my business done. And the nice thing is you're just as patient as when I was a puppy.

Maybe even a little more so. That's nice.

Sophie

My Pack

 Willow

 NuNu

 Flea

 Bit

Tinkerbell

I Wouldn't Sound Like That
By Tinkerbell

Brianna, sweetie. I know why you do it, pretending that I can talk human. You imitate my voice and say idiotic things in this high-pitched squeal. You think it's funny. And, you're very right, it could be funny. Hilarious. But it's not.

I've done it myself at those playdates with Muffy and White Fang, imitating your voice and mincing around. "Bad Tink," I whine, and they instantly recognize your voice. "Mom! Tink chewed up my retainer. Bad doggie." The girls and I were simply howling all day long, which you probably mistook for regular howling.

I even threw in a fairly good impression of your overbite. And just a reminder—if you wore your retainer instead of leaving it on the coffee table where anyone could find it, then you might just cure that problem.

But when you try to imitate me…let's just say, I thought a baby squirrel was in the room. Then I realized this was supposed to be my voice.

First off, I don't sound anything like that, even accounting for the translation. And second, you made me sound unforgivably dim and shallow, which I suppose you really can't help, can you?

I realize that you're all lonely and bored. You probably blame me for that. Well, I'm not the one who chased your boyfriend out of the house. Okay, yes, maybe I did. But mentally, dear, you chased him away the first time you refused to do his homework.

Boredom, however, is no excuse for holding me up like a hand puppet and wriggling my arms and squealing, "Ooh, I love my Brianna. Brianna is so pretty and nice and popular. All the boys love Brianna."

Not to mention going in and out of a bad Mexican accent whenever it suits you. You know perfectly well I was born in Boston. I am eleventh generation American, which goes back probably twenty years. Nineteen at least. So that could not possibly be how I would sound.

Tails up

Before You Knew Me

I see how you're looking—lying beside me on the dog bed, staring sadly into my eyes and wondering. What horribleness did I go through when that flood put my whole world under water? How did I wind up at that shelter? You feel sorry. So, if you really must know...

It was a clear morning, not a cloud in the sky. But I got up with a little vomiting and my human didn't want to leave me. So he took me into work. When I look back on that decision now... big mistake.

The first problem was "No Dogs Allowed." I know! I'm as offended as you, but I suppose they had their reasons. Everything went fine at first. He snuck me through the gate and down the elevator and I settled in under his desk for a few naps. No problem. Until later when his boss wandered onto the floor. Then there was a problem.

Our desk was far off in a corner, but his boss was headed straight our way. We didn't have much time and there was next to no place to hide. And by "next to no," I mean one: one place to hide. The locked-up room with the dangerous-looking letters on the door. I don't know how he got me into the locked-up room so fast, but he did. And that was the last time I saw him. Ever. I remember the last thing he said to me. "Be a good girl, okay? Don't make noise." Then he shut the door.

Of course I couldn't do it. The room was dark and musty. It wasn't too long (a second maybe) before I started whining and circling myself and trying to scratch at the door, which was tough because of the dark.

Pretty soon I'm knocking into buttons and switches and pulling down big levers. I went crazy. When someone finally opened up the door, it was too late. Lights were flashing and buzzers were buzzing. And the roar of water!

Oh. I suppose I should have said this earlier. My human worked at the Valley Dam. You know, the big dam on the water that had the horrible accident and flooded the whole valley and no one knows exactly what caused it. I don't know what caused it either, but...no, I really have no idea, but...

Fake out! Not a word of this is true. I'm playing with you, like when you pretend the tofu is meat. Just playing. You wanted a good story, so I just made it up. Like I would ever flood a valley!

My real story is pretty ordinary. I had a good life with a good family. When the flood came, they had to go away and couldn't take me. So I went into a shelter, and they never came back.

Thanks, by the way, for taking me in. I appreciate it.

 Moonbeam

WAITING BY THE TABLE

I can keep this up for hours. I'm not always so patient, you know, but when it comes to sitting by the table and staring up at you without blinking... "How does he do it?" you wonder. "How can Orson beg nonstop for so long?" It's all about concentration.

By the time you bring the plates to the table, I'm already in place, even though you're starting with salad. It doesn't excite you either; don't pretend. The most I can expect here is an oily crouton. But if I lose focus this early, you might think I'm not serious—seriously starving. So I stare like you're pushing green chicken legs around on the plate instead of those leaves.

Oh, speaking of chickens...why do humans throw away the best part of the leg? And why do I always find the most bones in the scary park on the corner? Also near construction sites. Those places are like chicken graveyards.

Oh, wait. We're up to the main course. How did that happen? Concentrate, Orson.

It's fish. I've been smelling it ever since you brought it home from the hot food store. There's also green stuff. And rice, which doesn't taste at all like dead maggots, despite the look. By the way, why does fish always smell like lemon? Do fish eat lemons, is that it? Or maybe people just put fish next to the lemons in the refrigerator. And don't even bring up how lemons got into the bottle of cleaning stuff. Why would anyone play a joke like that? And now that I mention it, lots of things smell like food that shouldn't, like candles and even the air when guests are coming.

Wait! What happened to the fish? That was fast. Okay, I'll help clean up. Please. Let me take the plates into the kitchen. I can preclean them before the dishwasher. Just let me help.

One last chance. Dessert in front of the TV. It's coming...it's coming...it's coming...it's...chocolate! Yes! I love chocolate. And it's not bad for me. Don't believe what that dog expert says. He lies. Is that expert a dog himself who loves the smell of chocolate? I don't think so. Please, please, please!

Okay, that's it. Tonight didn't work. No food. Fine. I'll just meet you here again tomorrow night. And this time I'll concentrate. Game on.

Puppies Know When They're Being Cute

Here's something a puppy will never tell you, partly because they're as dumb as a frog and wouldn't know where to start, and partly because they've got the attention span of another frog and would forget to tell you even if they could.

Puppies are like human babies. Being cute and sleeping and sucking on a nipple are the only things they're good at. Can they fetch or play dead? No. Can they lead blind people down the street? Just let them try. I dare you.

And they're calculating. You want to know why puppies start out with their eyes closed? So that when they open them, they'll look extra big and you'll say, "Ooh, honey, let's take it home."

Did I mention annoying? The way they're fascinated with socks like they've never eaten one before. The way they curl up against each other or stretch at weird angles, like they don't have a bone in their body. The way they love to play, even when they clearly don't know the rules. Do you think all this sweet behavior comes naturally? Yes! And that just makes it worse.

When you've spent as much time as me in a shelter, you know. It's the puppies who get adopted first. They bite you with their disposable teeth and pee in your hand and it's adorable. I was passed over for months and months. When someone finally picked me up and I bit her just a little and peed in her hand, no one said "adorable." There was this whole discussion about house-training and I was back inside for ages before I got another shot.

Plus, puppies think they're better than you, which is pretty rich coming from something so helpless. But it's true. They swat at your ears. They have no concept of personal space. All in all, a manipulative, annoying, too very cutesy breed, no matter what breed.

Except maybe Rottweilers.

Charlie

The Reason I Ate the Sofa

I know this is a sore subject. You've held this against me for like a coon's age, which I think is three to five years, unless the raccoon is trying to take a shortcut through our yard. Then it's less.

I'm not stupid. I knew it was a bad thing from the moment you walked into the house and said the word "bad" over and over again. By the way, why did you automatically think it was me? Not once did you turn and look at each other and ask, "Honey, did you eat the sofa?" No, you just assumed it was Axelrod.

Okay, it was Axelrod. But there's an explanation.

I didn't do it because I was angry that you were gone so long that day. I'm not the kind of dog who thinks about anger and revenge. Honestly. Revenge would require long-term thinking. I'm not good at that.

And it's not because I was bored. I actually started eating it just a few seconds after you walked out the door. Besides, I'm bored a lot. Sometimes I wish I had fleas or ticks because at least that would give me something to occupy my mind during those long, lonely stretches.

I think if you have to blame someone for the sofa, blame your-self. After all, you're the guys who brought home the really huge chew bone with the rawhide. Remember? That chew was almost as big as me at the time. And when I started eating it, you both laughed and took pictures.

It took me awhile to finish that bone. Then the sofa came into the house and how was I to know? That chew is made out of rawhide. And rawhide is like leather. And the sofa was made out of leather—or something kind of like leather. I thought you wanted me to go for it.

Honest mistake. Won't do it again. I guess the rule is, if you guys sit on it, it's not a chew.

Axelrod

MY DAYS AT THE JUNKYARD

There's no easy way to say this, so here goes. I lost my job with the cops.

Apparently there's some unwritten rule that a drug-sniffing dog should not enjoy the stuff he sniffs. So when they caught me with my teeth wrapped around some really primo weed, snarling and foaming... that was pretty much it.

Right away I got depressed. I was staying with Officer Simon, just sleeping on his couch and dreaming about those neighborhoods where we used to go on patrol. Then one day, Simon took me to this big yard full of junk. Well, they call it junk. But the stuff must be pretty good because it's my job to protect it.

This time my trainer was an interesting smelling guy named Loser. Sometimes they call him Dwayne, but mostly it's Loser. Loser actually likes it when I snarl and foam. And the games he teaches me are new—like tearing the leg off a dummy.

During the day, I laze around. Loser likes me to growl at everyone, but I always do it with my tail wagging, so they know I don't mean it.

At night, it's another story. It's just me, alone, protecting the big yard of junk. I take it seriously, since I already lost one job and I'm not even a year old. I patrol the whole fence, back and forth and around back again. And I never get distracted ever, except for the naps and talking to some other dogs way far away across the highway.

Oh, and the pot. I forgot to mention. Last night I found a stash of pot behind a wall in the trailer. I'm surprised I didn't find it before, since that used to be my job. I must have sniffed out dozens of stashes hidden inside trailer walls.

Needless to say, today I woke up late. Real late. Things were fuzzy, but to the best of my memory, I think Loser got fired. Him and the big boss were yelling at each other and pointing at the empty hole where the pot was. And then Loser took all his things and walked out, without even petting me good-bye.

At least I wasn't fired. And I made up my mind to work harder. Tonight I patrolled even more than usual and snarled at every single shadow. And it paid off. I just caught my first intruder.

It's true. Tonight this human was climbing over the spiky-topped fence, pretending to be all quiet and smell-less, and I caught him right at the bottom and bit his clothes and made him climb back up over the fence again.

I'm so proud of myself. I'm finally doing my job. I wish I could tell Loser about this. But he probably already knows, since it was him who was trying to climb over the fence.

SARGE

My Boys Don't Bite

First of all, let's not call it biting. They're nipping. They're just nipping you with these cute, tiny teeth that will fall out soon enough and get swallowed. Doesn't that make you feel better?

These are incredibly sharp tiny teeth, yes. But my boys don't mean to hurt.

And they only do it when they absolutely have to, like when they need attention. ("Mommy, mommy. Look at me or I'll break skin.") Or when they're showing you who's boss. Or when they're excited. Or playing. Or exploring. Or awake.

Your way of dealing with this in the past was to yell "ouch" in a loud voice and run away. That doesn't always work, especially since Mutt Junior thinks "ouch" means "good." How did this happen? I don't know. I'm not the one in charge of puppy-rearing; you made that very clear. But maybe, since it's a problem, you're finally ready to listen to some hints from their biological mother.

The best way to stop the nipping is to keep away from their teeth. Simple. Are you upset when Mutt Junior tugs at your pants? Don't wear pants.

Wear shorts. If you don't want Runt grabbing your shoelaces, don't wear shoes. Always keep your hands in your pockets or, better yet, high in the air. And you may want to have your own children live elsewhere for the next three months, just to keep those little fingers out of trouble. These precautions are fool-proof and should cut down on the nipping by almost half.

If you don't care enough to send your kids away, there are other things you can do, I suppose. No shouting and playing rough with the puppies. They shouldn't run or ride bikes through the house. No high-pitched squealing, espe-cially when their legs are already in the puppies' mouths. That just makes them bite harder.

There are many other solutions. You can choose to cover yourself in vinegar. My boys once ate a salad; they hate vinegar. Or you can spray them with water every time they bite, but don't put the spray on the mist setting. They like mist. Ooh, here's a better idea. Put vinegar in the bottle and you can spray everybody and everything. You like vinegar, right?

Personally, I just nip at the boys' ears and growl. They learn very quickly. Unfortunately, this approach is not for everyone. It just wouldn't be right for you to bite a dog. It isn't done.

Dimples

•I Like the Leash•

I know this sounds wrong, a dog actually liking the leash and being led around. But that's how I feel.

Some dogs may like the collar. Maybe they're used to it by now or they like the tinkly sound it makes. Some other dogs may pretend they're fond of leashes. But it's not the leash that gets them jumping up and down. It's going outside. The leash is, like, this necessary evil.

But I'm a country dog. Running free is normal. I don't think I even smelled a fence until I was grown. It must be like birds and flying. We all think it would be so great to fly and to be free like a bird, but when flying is the main thing you do all day...a bird probably thinks walking is pretty nice. You get to travel without having to flap all the time and watch out for windows.

So for me, there's nothing new about running free. The woods don't change much. Smells linger for weeks and weeks. The animals are all the same. And let's face it, one terrified raccoon up a tree is pretty much like another.

But the leash. There's excitement. It means that Toby is taking me somewhere I need to be controlled. A place with new smells. I get to see new people. And cars moving dangerously fast. And maybe sidewalks. I love sidewalks 'cause they lead right into stores. Did you ever smell a store? Unbelievable.

Then there's the fun of meeting new dogs. When you're both off leash, you gotta be careful. You prance around each other and sniff. Maybe somebody growls. But on a leash...you get to bark and pull and snarl and act nasty. But they're holding you back so no one gets hurt—except once when Toby twisted an ankle.

I guess my favorite time on a leash was this day when they let me smell a pair of handcuffs. Then I was off chasing down some man who ran away. Toby's

dad could barely hold onto me, I was so excited. When I finally found the guy, he was in this town hiding under a seat inside a movie theater.

That was my very first time in a movie theater. I just wish I could have stayed for the whole show.

Rufus T.

I RAISED YOUR KIDS

I know you're proud of how your kids turned out, but you never really thanked me for it. I'm a little resentful.

It was only a few months after I moved in that your twin babies arrived. I knew right off this wasn't a coincidence. The older one in the house helps care for the younger ones, right? I got the hint, and I took it seriously.

My first challenge was telling them apart. I kept getting them mixed up. But then Marcus started smelling different and getting bigger than Anna and it was easier.

For a few years, I was as smart as those two, maybe smarter. It took me a lot less time to get house-broken. Also walking. In fact, I'm the one who taught them. They didn't take their first stumbling steps running to you. No. They were running from me. A few weeks later and I was dragging them around with my tail.

For a while, I kept up with them in the brains department. We learned to spell around the same time. (Here's a clue: if you don't want me to know what W-A-L-K means, don't keep using it as a substitute for the word. "Let's take Bandana for a W-A-L-K." Didn't take long to figure that one out.)

I was also in charge of babysitting when you were in another room. And herding them. You never herded the kids at all, which seems to me like a parenting failure. How can you raise children without herding them around the house and the backyard? That became my responsibility.

When the twins started getting older and smarter than me, I was still teaching. They learned how to feed and water a dog, how to make it swallow a pill, and how to put a dog in a bathtub without drowning yourself or getting killed. Lessons that will help them throughout life.

I even helped with the important things, like kindness and patience. And knowing right from wrong. Like it's wrong to hide your poop in the corner, because someone will always find it eventually.

The Wind in My Ears

Something's always puzzled me. When we're driving in the car, really fast, why don't you stick your head out the window? I'm sure you've thought about it. I mean, I've been setting an example since forever, but you never tried it once.

I don't do it because I want to jump out. If I wanted out, why would I beg so much to get in the car in the first place? I wouldn't. And it's not because of the smells. Again, smelling the outside world is just as easy before I get in.

All right, part of it is the smell. But once we're moving... what could give off that much stink? Besides a skunk? And why would I want to smell a skunk? No, it's all about the sensation. The flapping of my flabby cheeks. All the air shooting into my two little nose holes so I can barely breathe. It's like...

It's like that time a few years back—when you were crying all the time for no real reason. You forgot to pet me for days. Remember that? Then you suddenly got better. It was around then. There was this day in your bathroom when you dropped a bunch of tiny little candies. And you got all mad and tried to stop me from going after them on the floor. And you scooped them up and counted them and looked around a whole lot. Well, I got me one of those candies when you weren't looking.

That was the best afternoon of my life. So peaceful and happy. I remember rolling around on my back and licking a light bulb and trying to bark like the cat. You probably didn't notice. For days and days I kept trying to find another one of those little candies. Later on, I did find one, but it was different, and I fell right to sleep for maybe a week.

Anyway, sticking your head out of a car is like that candy. Not the second candy, the first. You should really try it. Not the candy, the wind. It's great.

Sophie

My Pack

 Willow

 NuNu

 Flea

 Bit

Tinkerbell

My Life in Your Purse
By Tinkerbell

Margo, dear. FYI.

Being carried around in that purse is kind of a mixed bag. (That's probably clever, but I'm not really sure.) What I mean is sometimes it's fun, like when you sneak me into a bar and I drink a few sips of your melon swizzle. And sometimes it's bad, like when you're swinging me and the Gucci at the head of some boyfriend. That gives me a thumping headache, especially after a melon swizzle.

But sometimes it's very bad in a way that defies explanation. Let me explain.

Last week, just as I was quietly rummaging around in Brianna's tote, looking for some Tic Tacs, the two of you got into this fight. It was about one of you acting like a slut, which could have been just about any recent fight.

Before I could even stick my head out and take sides, Brianna grabbed the tote and slammed out the door. I thought about telling her I was in there, but my mouth was full of Tic Tacs.

After a lot of bumping around, Brianna finally stopped. Suddenly I could smell peppermint and cherry, and I knew just where we were. Her favorite store. The one where she buys things when she's mad, not the one where she buys things when she's happy.

I don't know why I stayed quiet. Maybe I was waiting for her to reach inside so I could surprise her with a fierce growl. She's always so funny when I growl.

But when things got a little too quiet, I poked my head out, just to get my bearings. The tote and I were sitting in one of those tiny rooms where Brianna goes to try on clothing. Brianna wasn't there but I could hear her talking to a salesgirl somewhere, asking her if this dress made her look as slutty as her mother.

They were out there awhile, chatting about mothers. But you know me, I get bored. And uncomfortable. It's not fun getting bounced around. And that's when I saw the cute little blouse on the bench right next to me. It didn't take more than a minute to grab it and drag it back into the tote, where it would make the absolutely nicest pillow for the ride back home.

So…I'm not exactly sure how Brianna got arrested or why. But just as we were leaving the store, there were bells going off and people yelling. Lots of drama, just like home. Anyway, I guess my point is it's not always smart to carry me around in your purse.

On the other hand, I finished all the Tic Tacs and my breath smelled great.

Tails up

Why Do I Eat Grass?

Let me tell you about grass eating. First, it's not because I don't get enough veggies. Get that theory out of your head. Every time you see me munching on the lawn doesn't mean you have to feed me another salad. I also eat garbage. Does that mean I don't get enough garbage? Or dog poop. Am I missing some dog poop in my diet? In some ways, I'm like a crawling baby. I will eat just about anything that fits in my mouth.

But still you look out your window, past the stained-glass rainbow, and there I am, munching like a cow. So I guess your next question is, "Does it taste good?" Compared to garbage and poop, it's not great. But I don't get that stuff every day. Compared to my regular vegan diet? Pretty delicious.

I know what your nutritionist says: grass is good medicine. I eat it because I have an upset tummy and it helps me to throw up whatever bad thing is inside. She thinks this way because a lot of dogs throw up after eating grass. But what if the truth is just the opposite? Go with me here. What if we eat the grass out of sheer stupidity and it gives us an upset tummy, and then we throw up? Pretty interesting, huh? The first theory makes us so smart that we go out and find our own medicine. The next theory makes us so dumb that we'll eat something we know will make us sick. Why would we do that? I don't know. It's kind of like you drinking wheatgrass juice every morning. Oh, by the way, why do you drink wheatgrass juice every morning? I've seen the face you make. Ugh.

Of course, there could be other reasons I eat grass. Maybe I'm hungry. Or maybe I discovered some cat urine on that particular patch, like a tasty dressing.

But I suppose I should be honest with you. Dogs are supposed to be honest. The real reason I eat grass...it's something that you probably wouldn't guess, a really strange reason, but true. Something you'd never guess in a hundred dog years. The real reason why I... chipmunk! Gotta go.

Chipmunk, chipmunk, chipmunk, chipmunk, chipmunk, chipmunk, chipmunk...

☮ Moonbeam

I LIVE TO SERVE

I've been going through a few jobs lately. Like when they tried to train me to be a search and rescue dog. That happened right after my days at the junkyard and I may have gotten the training signals mixed up. Or my next job. I got this horrible ear infection right when they were teaching me how to help that guy who couldn't hear.

This time I'm not going to screw up. They call me a service dog and I even get a uniform, a vest with a handle on top that kind of makes me look like a suitcase. My boss is a woman named Darla. Her petting skills are a little clumsy since that's her main problem, something with her hands. But that's my job now.

Darla took some getting used to, mainly because she's bossy. Half the words out of her mouth are some kind of command. "Light switch," "Bring it here," "Back up. Not that far. Ouch. Help." I don't really remember "ouch" from my training, but she says it a lot.

At first I thought she was lazy, like Loser when he taught me how to bring him beer out of the cold box. One time, as a test, I pretended I didn't hear when Darla said,

"Open door." She said it over and over. Finally she did manage to get out of the bathroom, so she's not helpless. But I guess it goes faster when I do it.

We get along pretty good now. It's like a game. Sometimes it's "Walkies." Sometimes it's "Simon Says"...you know, when she gives me the same commands Officer Simon used to. But mostly it's "Fetch," endless, endless games of fetching this or that.

There are great parts too. Don't get me wrong. When she cooks, I pretend to be clumsy. Then I clean up the floor. And I get to go into these magical places where they bring you food and dozens of people sit in chairs and drop crumbs on the floor.

Oh, and she dresses me up like her. I take a hat from a shelf and we put it on my head and go for a ride in the car. It's great. I sit right beside her and we get to drive in the fast lane where most of the other cars don't go...Although today we did get stopped by a car with flashing lights and a police officer. He seemed angry about my hat. He yelled a lot and wrote us a ticket.

Hope I didn't do anything wrong. I need this job.

SARGE

I TRIED TO LOSE WEIGHT- ONCE

I miss the baby carriage. I miss the game we used to play when you guys would squeeze me in there, cover me with a blanket, and push me into the food store. You would pretend I was a baby and laugh. I loved it when you took food from the shelves and put it into a big cart just inches from the carriage. I would squirm and squirm. Not because I didn't like the game. But because...you know, being close to food.

So, when we played the game the other day and I squirmed and squirmed and the baby carriage broke, and everything flew out of the cart, and the man in the store yelled at you for no reason...that was when I knew I had to lose weight.

I used to think that losing weight had something to do with eating. It seemed simple. But after watching the two of you for years and years, I realize that a diet is very complicated.

The first trick seems to be not to eat when people are looking. I don't know how many times you sat down and ate a little plate of vegetables. And then, in the middle of the night, one of you would sneak into the kitchen and eat half a tub of ice cream. And then later on the other one would do exactly the same thing. And in the morning, you would pretend that there had never been any ice cream at all and we would go to the store again with the baby carriage.

So this was my plan. At the very next dinnertime, I refused to get excited. It took all my self-control, but I did it. I sniffed carefully at the bowl, then slowly ate about half the kibble and pushed the bowl away. You were stunned, I remember. You called the other one over and talked and talked. Then you pushed the bowl toward me again. But I just walked away.

That night, I snuck out onto the balcony and ate half the charcoal briquettes from the bag by the hibachi.

The next day at breakfast, I did it again. Half a bowl. (And three great-tasting diapers from the neighbor's garbage.) That afternoon, you took me to the doctor. But all he did was put a cotton swab up my butt and feel my stomach and send us home.

That night, you cooked for me. Livers and chicken and beef. And even with all your cooking skill, it was still great-tasting, and I ate and ate. And that was the end of my plan. And I think I gained a pound.

I guess the lesson from all this would be that diets don't work. I'll remember that.

Orson

Go Ahead, Blame the Dog

A dog always gets blamed. Like when Toby's grandma farts and everyone looks my way. Or someone digs up a prize-winning bush 'cause it was blocking the hole at the bottom of the fence...okay, that was me. But I get blamed a lot.

So maybe you can see how nervous I was on that day when I took a big poop and Toby and his pals came after me and picked it up in a paper bag. This is not normal for Toby, you know. And from the way they looked at the bag and laughed, I knew they were getting set to pull a prank and that my poop was going to be in the middle of it.

I hung out with them all afternoon, just to see what was up. And sure enough, when no one but me was looking, Toby put the bag on Crazy Harriet's porch, right on top of the doormat. Then he lit a match to the bag and knocked on the door.

One thing you need to know about Crazy Harriet. She's not from here. You can tell by how she talks. I don't know what's crazy about her either, except that she lives by her-self and no one likes her.

By now, Toby is running away laughing, and the poop is catching fire. Inside the house, Crazy Harriet is coming slowly to the door, calling out, "Who's there?" And all I can think is that it's my poop that's flaming and I'm going to get blamed.

I still don't know why I did what I did. But I raced right up on that porch and bit into the doormat with the bag still on it and dragged everything right off the porch and down the stairs to some-where safe.

Another thing you need to know about Crazy Harriet. Her porch is really, really close to Toby's fence, which is kind of old and dry. Toby and his friends stopped laughing when they saw me grab the doormat. And they really stopped laughing when the fence caught fire.

So everyone is blaming me again, even though I couldn't light a fire if my life depended on it. I would say I was in the doghouse, but I can't because the doghouse was kind of attached to the fence.

At least Toby didn't get in trouble. And now I get to spend time with Crazy Harriet. When I'm not out hunting, she lets me sit in her house, listening to musical shows on the stereo. She shows me magazine pictures of this place called New York, full of big build-ings and fancy people, and you know what? It looks fantastic.

Rufus T.

I Don't Understand Elevators

You probably think I'm totally relaxed and confident, like the world is my kibble. I amble through life with my tongue hanging out. Life is good. But sometimes I do get anxious.

Hard to believe, right?

But there are an awful lot of mysteries in my world. Like, why is the sky wet sometimes? Why does the TV go on and off when I chew on the plastic bone? And that little room. You go inside and the door slides shut and when it opens again, we're some-place completely else. Whoa! What is that?

The first time you took me into one of those rooms, it rumbled and shook. Then the door opened and we were in a new place, which I did not expect at all. I tried not to let it show, like this was normal. But for a minute I wasn't even thinking about if there was a ball in your pocket. That's how thrown I was.

This room. I guess it's like a car inside a building, right? It makes noise and moves and I never know where we're going to get out, except with a car it's usually someplace outside—and with this room it's usually someplace with a hallway or desks.

And it's not the same as a closet, right? Because a closet has clothes in it. And it doesn't rumble. And it only takes you back to the room you were already in.

Someday I'll figure it out. I already figured out glass, which is not exactly air. It's thick air that you can't walk through. And I figured out screen doors, which are like fences you can't see until you're halfway through them.

I guess I don't need to understand everything. Things will be good even if I don't know how they work. A door will open and it'll be some-place with a treat or a toy or a nice sofa. I can just trust in the universe to provide.

And by universe, I mean you.

AXELROD

All Alone in the World

Here is something every dog knows from birth: a puppy left alone is a dead puppy. Maybe that's not so true, but at one time it was. And we still feel it. It's scary when your pack abandons you in the woods to get picked off by some eagle or snake. Of course, the woods we're talking about now have a lot of sofas and chairs and rugs. And are indoors. But it's still perfectly normal for my boys to howl and scratch and tremble whenever you leave the house.

True, they're never really alone. They have each other—and me. But ever since you took over the mother job—no hard feelings—they treat me more like a sister. No one listens to a sister. In fact, sometimes I even howl and scratch with them.

I suppose you want to cure them—that's my guess—but you're not doing such a good job. You started by feeling guilty every time you walked out the door. (Sure, we can smell fear. But guilt is even stronger smelling—kind of musty and sick.) You made such a fuss, kissing them and leaving plenty of treats and toys. No wonder they freaked.

You want my best advice? Sneak out. Don't let them know you're gone. Half the time when you're here, they're asleep or in another room or don't really care. So just pretend you're in another room. Put on the TV, with some TV voice that sounds like yours. Or maybe close the door to the bathroom. It would be good if you could put a voice in the bathroom too—maybe a voice that grunts every now and then and says, "Don't scratch the door. Can't I have a moment's peace?" That should do the trick.

Oh, and you're going to need a few human-looking dolls to place on the bed or the living-room couch. Be sure to rub them all over your body right before you leave too, just to get the smell right.

Or you could just never leave. That might be the easiest solution.

Dimples

WHY DO I CIRCLE?

I may not be human smart, but at least I'm interested in life's big, big questions, like how the house can be dark and then be suddenly full of light, all in a split-second. You, on the other paw, are often caught up in the small things, like, "Why do dogs circle themselves three times before lying down?" Now, a more curious mind might think, "Wow, dogs can count to three." But not you. No, it's the circling part that gets your attention.

Well, I suppose I could ask you about your own behavior, like why do you fluff up a pillow right before you squash it with your head? Or why do you look back and forth and back and forth before crossing a street, even when there's a cat on the other side and you're just wasting time?

Back to the circling. You have to understand that sleeping is important. Crucial. It ranks right up there with the two or three other things in our lives. So we have to properly prepare. First thing we do is circle around once, to establish our territory. "This is my spot, and no one else can have it."

We do the second circle to check the ground for predators and other things, like snakes and scorpions. Of course I've never seen a scorpion, but it's still in my brain, hardwired for no real reason, like you. You're hardwired to pull all the blankets to your side of the bed, even when you're not cold.

Circle number three is for comfort, to tamp down the tall grasses or the mud hole in the jungle—except in modern life we're tamping down a dog bed or the kitchen floor. It's kind of the same reason why I scratch the sofa before I even make my first circle, because… um, forget it. I never scratch the sofa. Ever.

Sometimes I'll even do a fourth circle, to check the direction of the wind. (I like to sleep with my back to the heating vent.) Doing a fourth circle is very rare, although I'll often do a fifth circle instead. And if you ever see me doing a sixth circle, it's because I forgot where I was and had to start over.

I hope this explains it.

I Like the Spa

Yesterday I went for the very first time. I guess they thought I was finally old enough and deserved some pampering. Also, it was probably a reward for becoming so perfectly house-trained in so short a time. Plus I had fleas.

A lot of dogs don't like the spa, mainly the ones who hate water and baths and separation. But from the second you walk in, there are all these amazing scents. Oh sure, there's the smell of fear. But even stronger is the tar shampoo and the green apple rinse and all these other smells that don't ever happen in real life.

All types of dogs come there. Some of them are kind of dumb and only want to talk about balls and pull toys and swimming. It's surprising how you can pass by someone in a car and chat through the open window and they're fine. But when you actually try to talk to them...no one home.

For the first little while, you sit in these private cages. But that doesn't stop you from sharing some gossip back and forth. Like who is starting to smell her age. And who's been seen out and about with a new walker. And who needs to get her anal glands emptied. I mean, really. You can't just rub it on the floor. It's not working.

Next they bathe you and groom you. And still everyone

talks—about what they had for breakfast or what they said this morning to the dog in the yard on the corner. I pay special attention when the subject turns to boys. I just started noticing boys, and every day I seem to get more interested. A lot of the girls are more attracted to the boys with testicles. Maybe I'll feel that way some day. But for right now, I go for someone with good hair and nice teeth and a growl that's not too threatening.

By the time I finally left, I had my nails clipped and my ears cleaned and a nice pretty bow in my hair. I was the prettiest one there. Everyone said so. And as I went strutting out the door, I couldn't help thinking, "Gabby, you are not a puppy anymore. From now on, you are an adult. A real grown-up bitch."

♡ Gabby

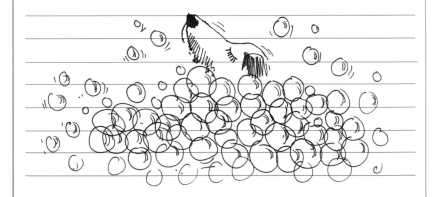

Why Do We Wag Our Tails?

I know what you're thinking. "Out of the seven dogs running around the house, why is Charlie answering this question? He barely has a tail." I would just like to point out that this isn't my fault. I had a tail once but it disappeared, like the balls between my legs—also not my fault. I do have a little stub and, you know me, I wag it when I'm happy—or after a bath when I'm wagging everything.

Okay, back to the question. Unless you're very dim—I mean golden retriever dim—your real question isn't why do we wag, but why do we wag to show happiness. I mean, monkeys don't wag their tails when they're happy. Birds don't. And cats—well, they're never happy, not in any meaningful way.

It's a good question. Why don't we just bark instead of wag? We bark for everything else. Or clap our paws together or wiggle our ears? (I still have my entire ears by some miracle. Thank you.) It's a good question. Let me give it some thought...right after my nap.

Auuuuuw! Good nap. Now, where was I? Yawning? Why do dogs yawn? You tell me, people, why do you yawn? No, that's not right. Napping. Why do we nap? Well, why do you...No! Wagging the tail.

Yes. I've been giving this a lot of thought.

I think, ages ago, we all used to bark instead of wagging,

but it got too noisy. Dogs are naturally happy, and with all that happy barking, no one was getting any sleep. And barking probably didn't help when we were out hunting, trying to sneak up on things. "Look, guys, a squirrel. Hooray! Never mind, he's gone."

We had to come up with something else, and quick. And we only had so many body parts to work with. Then some genius invented wagging the tail and it stuck. Mothers have been teaching it to pups ever since. "Don't bark, sweetie. It's annoying. Do this."

So now we can all show happiness quietly, while watching TV or listening to music or while sneaking up on that sleepy cat who's not smart enough to figure out how to wag his tail. Life is good.

Charlie

THE SEVEN RULES OF FOOD

1. I know when another dog gets a treat and I don't. Even when I'm not there, like in another room or in a house down the street. Don't ask how I know. Just don't try it again.

2. In a similar vein. When you give me a treat and another dog comes over and you give him one...if more than three seconds have gone by, then I don't remember. You owe me a second treat.

3. More than once, and for no reason, you push back my breakfast and dinnertime by one hour. This goes on for months and months. All the meals are exactly one hour late, until you finally realize your mistake and get my feeding schedule back on track. This is very annoying. Please stop.

4. Human food is better than dog food. Want to see me get even more excited about dinner? Take a few bites out of my bowl. The fact that you're eating it automatically makes it better.

5. Except for grapes. No more grapes. You gave me this major punishment once when I knocked over the

bowl on the coffee table and tried to eat them before you could stop me. How was I to know? You acted like they were good. I've never been so disappointed.

6. I don't see you being forced to shake hands before you get a snack. Okay, sure, I'll still shake hands. It just seems like a double standard.

7. I don't care what my treats are shaped like. They can be tiny pork chops or sausages or even things that look like bow ties, which I guess might also look like bones from a cow if you use your imagination. It doesn't matter. I barely look at them anyway.

Orson

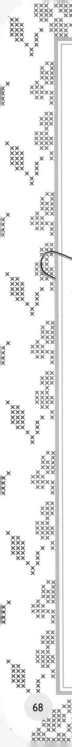

S

Why Am I Barking?

Remember that time when the kids were small and they went camping in the backyard? You let me sleep with them in the tent for their protection and also because I kept scratching to go out back. Then in the middle of the night, I started going crazy like a poodle. Katie woke up and thought she saw a man climbing the fence. And you guys ran outside and called the police. And they stopped some man nearby. And I barked extra hard and they took him away. And you kept saying what a good girl I was and gave me a chewy, without me having to beg for it. Remember?

Turns out I made that up.

In my defense, I wasn't faking. The first couple of barks were real. Maybe I heard an owl. Or a leaf fell and I wanted you to know. Maybe it was the voices in my head. But then Brian started shouting and Katie started screaming. Then the lights went on in the house and everyone was pointing. I got caught up in the moment.

It's not like I ever gave you any reason to think I was reliable. How many times do I bark wildly at the door and no one shows up? No mailman. No next-door neighbor trying to sneak past the front gate with her little rat dog. Of course, sometimes I am right, but then so is a broken clock. Or a poodle.

I'm not saying this is your fault. Just like it wasn't the fault of the poor man who was out walking that night. Things happen. But maybe it's just a little self-centered of you to think that every time I bark, it has something to do with you. I'm not always trying to protect you. Sometimes I'm just saying, "Hey." Or, "I just farted."

Lately I've taken to barking just to remind everyone that I'm still around. The same way old humans do. "Hey, look at me. I can still make noise and be important."

You know? Sometimes I dream about that night in the backyard. Snuggling with the kids and the big moon and all the excitement. That was the best.

Sophie

My Pack

 Willow

 NuNu

 Flea

 Bit

Tinkerbell

Tinkerbell's Pet Peeves
By Tinkerbell

I guess this is mainly to Brianna, but also to Margo. Frankly, you're both equally irritating. Congratulations!

All Chihuahuas do not look alike. I was once in the spa with my grandmother, and some stupid groomer said we looked like twins. Twins? My grandmother? She must be five years older. You humans all look alike. Okay? You and your grandmother. How do you like that?

I hate it when you pose me with all your stuffed animals and take pictures and then ask strangers which animal is real.

I don't think I'm big, so stop saying it. "See how fierce Tink is? She thinks she's a big dog." I'm not an idiot, okay? I know I'm tiny. The only reason I go after big dogs is so that they won't want to go after me. Kind of like you and boys.

I am not a kitten, so stop putting me on the piano and taking videos.

Why do you expect me to come every time you say my name? Do you come to me every time I bark? Okay, that may not be the best comparison, since I do bark a lot more than you say my name. But that's not my point.

I don't get the big deal when we go to the spa and you treat me to a special doggie massage. A massage is exactly the same as being petted, except they stop after an hour and you have to tip them.

The sign on the fence? "Property Protected by Chihuahua." Is that necessary? Why do you have to warn people ahead of time?

I have legs, dear. I can walk. I don't have to be carried around in backpacks or Chanel bags or your boney arms. Also, I can get around a dusty living room just fine without you putting me on top of the Roomba. That little machine makes me dizzy.

 Tails up

I Got a Secret Life

Toby's at that age where he's spending more time with his pals. Me, I'm spending more time with Crazy Harriet. She's home a lot, cooking and writing things down. Maybe she's a cook or a writer, I don't know. I just sit by her side listening to music and looking at magazines.

I don't know how it started, but Harriet somehow got me into truffles. I remember one day in the kitchen, she brings out this jar and sticks my nose in it and says "truffles." Oh, wait...I guess that's how it started.

Next thing you know, we're in the woods, sniffing around tree roots. It takes me awhile because they're very hard to find. But when I do find one, Harriet makes quite the fuss and digs them up and we go back home wagging our butts. It turns out truffles is food.

I remember when Harriet first came, she had a pig that went hunting truffles with her. From what I've been able to piece together, the pig stole too much of the truffles maybe and got cranky and old and...anyway, Harriet says that truffles go great with pork. It's true. She cooked up a little ham steak from her freezer. Delicious.

The food at Harriet's was tasty. But I felt guilty. I mean, I was ignoring Toby and his family. What kind of loyal dog is that? Then I thought back to all the dinners at their house. Not tasty. So I felt sorry for them about their food. And guilty. And a little lonely.

That's when I decided to go home. I would be a good dog and live with them because they're my people. But I also wanted to bring them something. It took me all day to find it and dig it out. Then I had to wash it off with my tongue. But when I finished, I had the biggest, tastiest truffle ever seen. Harriet would have loved it, but no, she couldn't have it.

That night, I snuck back home and into the kitchen. It was good being home. There was no way I could explain the truffle. So I just balanced myself on the stove and plunked the whole thing into the stew. And, of course, that's when Toby's mom came in and saw me. Right away, she fished it out and smelled it and announced that it was a big ugly turd.

Later, when they untied me from the doghouse, I went right back to Crazy Harriet. She welcomed me inside and gave me a pillow and started playing the music from *Annie*, nice and loud.

I hate to say it, but sometimes a stranger's place can feel more like home.

Rufus T.

I Like When You Go Away

Maybe I should be upset when you guys go away. I know you're upset. I can tell by the whimpery voice and the hugs and the extra treats. That can mean only two things. Either you're going on a trip or you're having my balls removed. Lately it's been trips.

But I'm in good hands when you're gone. You take me next door to Bernie's. He's my best bud in the world, next to you. Bernie likes when I spend a few days with him. I watch him through the slats in the fence, taking the small, delicate stuff out of his house to the garage and bringing in the plastic stuff that we like to play with. I get so excited. I call out to him, "Bernie...Bernie...Bernie... Bernie...Bernie..." Just like that for hours.

It's not that Bernie's games are better. But he mixes it up. Take "Food in the Sofa." At home, it's simple. You hide the popcorn and the nuts and the smelly spilled drinks. Then during the night I claw away at the cushions until I find them. But Bernie covers his sofa in this plastic. Makes all the difference. I really have to rip and claw until I finally get through to the cushions. And he doesn't leave food on the counter in plain sight. Not

Bernie. He hides it behind cabinet doors, where I have to work for it.

Plus, there's always something a bit different since my last visit. Like the rug in his hallway. The old one was a lot of fun to play with, but the new one looks like it could be fun too. I'm keeping my eye on it.

You probably don't believe this about Bernie. To you, he's this shy, quiet guy who wouldn't yell at a fly. But I bring out his fun side. The longer I stay, the more excited he gets. And louder. After a couple of days, this guy who never raises his voice...running around and yelling "no" at the top of his lungs and playing tag with me and the newspaper. It's like all the fun we used to have at obedience school. Remember?

One more story and I'll stop.

On my last visit, I was looking around for the wax fruit. It's one of our games, but he makes it harder every time. First the bowl was on the coffee table, then on a desk, then on a counter. This time, nowhere in sight. Then some morning, I'm nosing around the basement and there it is, on a high shelf, under a pile of rags.

There's not much left, but I pick a wax banana. Two bites. Then I run up the stairs and look for a good place to vomit. Hardwood floors? No. Bathroom tiles? Don't be silly. I'm heaving now, getting dangerously close. Kitchen? No. There it is. Finally. Bernie's new rug! Yes.

Nothing like a rug.

AXELROD

I'm Not a Strict Vegan

I like vegetables. They hold the meat together. It's a nice break, and I wind up with these great, smelly farts. But it was kind of a new idea when you took the meat out totally and left just the stuff holding it together.

I honestly thought it was a mistake. I kept trying to find the cow or chicken or pig. But you explained over and over—even though you knew I didn't understand, even though I did. Killing is wrong. It wastes a lot of nature and hurts the world's karma and a bunch of other things I stopped paying attention to because I'm so hungry for meat.

I happen to know nature a little better than you, having lived there, and it doesn't really mind getting killed. Not really. I mean, what choice does it have?

Killing seems natural to me. For example, I love chasing pigeons. And it's not because we're playing tag. Look at my favorite toy, the squeaky squirrel. It's made to look like a squirrel. I track it across the lawn and attack. And those squeaks add to the fun, especially when I get them going fast, like he's in a crazy panic. And then I stop. And the squirrel stops squeaking. Doesn't get better than that.

I dream about meat now. I can't even have eggs and cheese, which is confusing because...why can't I have them? They're not meat. They're the things that meat doesn't want and leaves behind. Look, I know this is important to you. But I don't try to make you live by my rules—mainly because I don't have any.

So every day I gobble up the soy and the yeast and the olive oil. It beats starving. And then you test my pee. You dip in these little strips, like the ones you use in the pool, just to make sure that my stomach is fine. Like I'm some kind of living hot tub.

I would really be desperate if your boyfriend didn't slip me some real meat now and then. He cooks what he calls his "famous vegan" meatloaf. You keep asking him to make it, and you yourself let me nibble on the leftovers. So, technically I guess it's you who slips me the meat. Because, although I never personally killed a cow, I certainly know what it tastes like.

☮ Moonbeam

THE INTRUDER

It happens all the time. A man with a bag and a uniform walks up to the house. This is not the guy who has the bag and the uniform and the white beard. Him I've only seen a few times at parties. He's okay. No, this other one comes at the same time almost every day, whether you're home or not.

I knew he was trouble from the moment I saw him through the window. I started out treating him like any other arrival. "Hello? Hello? Identify yourself. Hello?" He didn't identify himself. In fact, he didn't get any closer than that little box by the porch rail. He stood there for a few seconds—then simply turned around and retreated. I'd won! He was obviously scared off by my questions, or maybe just my tone of voice.

But the next day, he showed up again. I must not have been forceful enough. This time I yelled even louder. "Please go away, sir—or I will be forced to tear your throat out." Again my strategy worked. Coward. He got no farther than the little box then fled for his life.

Now every day he tries. I'm not quite sure what he's trying. But he never succeeds, because if he succeeded then he wouldn't keep coming back, would he? No, he wouldn't.

Sometimes when you and I are on the street, I see this guy

lurking around the neighborhood, probably just waiting until we're out of the house. He says hello to you like a friend. That doesn't fool me. If he was a friend, he would come into the house and visit and pet me. This guy keeps his distance. He tries to smile, but I know a nervous smile when I see one. Once he handed me a treat, which I took without making any promises. I mean, who can trust a man who bribes you and carries the faint smell of pepper spray in his right jacket pocket?

There have been other visitors in uniform, and they turn out to be okay. They ring the bell and talk to you and hand you packages. But it's this one guy we have to keep our eye on.

I'll let you know if I ever catch him.

Bandana

Training My Boys

I can't help seeing that you have a wee problem. Now, far be it from me to give advice...after all, you did take over the job of raising my sons. Oh, all right, I'll give advice. But only because you're crying in your sleep and starting to shed. The last thing this house needs is a shedding human—on top of three shedding dogs and the smell of pee in every rug.

Speaking of rugs...whose idea was it to put down a new rug at exactly the same time I had puppies? Dogs absolutely love a new rug. I can barely stop myself from going on it; it feels so right.

Did you forget how hard this training is? Then your memory's worse than mine, and I can't remember the last time I had a treat. A week ago? I guess you thought it was easy because every time you take the boys out, they go. But they also go every time you don't take them out. Their insides are just like little sponges—cheap, nasty sponges that dribble everywhere and seem to spill more than they take in.

You can't yell at them, you know. They don't

understand. They know you're mad, but they're thinking, "Okay. Bad dog. I'll try to figure out what I did wrong just as soon as I pee and feel a little better. Oops, what do you know! Poop and pee. Now I feel great."

Your main strategy seems to be the old "newspaper on the kitchen floor." I remember this. It's how I learned to pee on newspapers. And not just in the kitchen. On the front porch. In the living room after you read them. In the special garbage can where you put them. It took me years before I could look at a paper without feeling all warm inside.

You were so desperate to get them trained that you even left the kitchen door open so they could go outside when they needed. Unfortunately, this allowed the neighbor's cat to come inside one day. Not a good idea, for you or the cat. I'm sure you blame that whole kitchen fiasco on my boys. But if you sniff carefully—the smell is still there—you'll notice that there's definitely some cat pee mixed in. Vinegar, by the way, is great for covering this up.

Did I say I had advice? Sorry. Just thought I'd gloat. These guys are your job.

Dimples

Beauty and the Dog

Today is my very first beauty pageant. I'm so excited.

I know. Lots of dogs hate them. These shows are totally demeaning and stressful and promote some false ideal of beauty...blah, blah, bark, snarl, blah...who cares! You know who makes the biggest stink about them? Mutts. Loser mutts who would never be allowed inside a beauty pageant in a million-trillion years.

My mom and dad both did pageants, I'll have you know. My dad still does them, even at his age, which I think is four. They promote good habits and self-confidence. Plus they're great places to pick up well-bred females. He laughs when he says this, but my mom doesn't laugh.

Pageants are well respected in our doghouse. So, when they started grooming me alongside my dad and teaching me to prance—well, I knew this was it. I did everything right too. I ate fish oil from the trash for a glossy coat—and motor oil from the driveway, to help me vomit and stay greyhound-thin. And I learned who not to bite at a pageant. Apparently, you're not supposed to bite anyone.

Today, things started early and went quick. A bath and a

grooming and a ride in the car—but no head out the window, 'cause we just had our hair done. Before you know it, we're there. Dad is taken away to do his own thing and I'm left with a bunch of kids my age. My competition, so to speak. That's my way of saying I'm so much better. Just look at them.

It's true. You may think all show dogs are alike, but look. You see? I'm just a little thinner than the others—thank you, motor oil. My ears are a tad smaller. And my nose. For a dachshund, it's downright perky. But what really sets me apart are my legs. They're not nearly as short and stubby—especially with how I learned to walk on my toes. I can make them look pretty lanky, almost like an Afghan's.

Oops. Here comes the judge. He looks so impressed. I love that frown on his face. Gotta go!

P.S. The mutts were right. Pageants are stupid. They're demeaning and full of stupid judges and I'm never going to do it again. Never, never, never.

♡ Gabby

HOSPITALS ARE FUN

Before working for Darla, I was never in a hospital. Now we go a lot. The last time was after a game of "I'm Ignoring You." That's when I'm tired and Darla yells at me to do something, usually at night, and I muster up just enough energy to hide. This time her feet found me before her eyes, and she finally got to use that emergency button around her neck.

So we spent a few days at the hospital. I got to live there too, since my job is to help Darla, even when she's mad and tries to push me away. She can push very hard for a lady with a broken leg, and no one seemed to mind when I left her room and started wandering the halls.

One of the places I found was this big room with a TV and a whole lot of sick people. From the second I walked in, they were happy to see me—unlike some people. (I mean Darla.) I came right up to a little girl sitting all alone. She stared at me for a long while. Then she just put her arms around my neck and hugged. It was the first time I'd been hugged in quite some time.

The rest of the day was more of the same. Some of them petted and some hugged. Some just looked. The old people talked

Barnes & Noble Booksellers #2565
3111 South Veterans Pkwy
Springfield, IL 62704
217-546-9440

STR:2565 REG:007 TRN:5789 CSHR:Ann G

Things Your Dog Doesn't Want You to Know
9781402263286   T1
(1 @ 12.99)   12.99

Subtotal   12.99
Sales Tax T1 (8.000%)   1.04
TOTAL   **14.03**
VISA   **14.03**
  Card#: XXXXXXXXXXXXX2188
  Expdate: XX/XX
  Auth: 029111
  Entry Method: Swiped

A MEMBER WOULD HAVE SAVED   1.30

Thanks for shopping at
Barnes & Noble

101.28A   07/20/2012 06:04PM

CUSTOMER COPY

Return Policy

<u>With a sales receipt or Barnes & Noble.com packing slip</u>, a full refund in the original form of payment will be issued from any Barnes & Noble Booksellers store for returns of undamaged NOOKs, new and unread books, and unopened and undamaged music CDs, DVDs, and audio books made within 14 days of purchase from a Barnes & Noble Booksellers store or Barnes & Noble.com with the below exceptions:

A store credit for the purchase price will be issued (i) for purchases made by check less than 7 days prior to the date of return, (ii) when a gift receipt is presented within 60 days of purchase, (iii) for textbooks, or (iv) for products purchased at Barnes & Noble College bookstores that are listed for sale in the Barnes & Noble Booksellers inventory management system.

Opened music CDs/DVDs/audio books may not be returned, and can be exchanged only for the same title and only if defective. NOOKs purchased from other retailers or sellers are returnable only to the retailer or seller from which they are purchased, pursuant to such retailer's or seller's return policy. Magazines, newspapers, eBooks, digital downloads, and used books are not returnable or exchangeable. Defective NOOKs may be exchanged at the store in accordance with the applicable warranty.

Returns or exchanges will not be permitted (i) after 14 days or without receipt or (ii) for product not carried by Barnes & Noble or Barnes & Noble.com.

Policy on receipt may appear in two sections.

Return Policy

<u>With a sales receipt or Barnes & Noble.com packing slip</u>, a full refund in the original form of payment will be issued from any Barnes & Noble Booksellers store for returns of undamaged NOOKs, new and unread books, and unopened and undamaged music CDs, DVDs, and audio

YOU MAY ALSO LIKE...

Stupid Conservatives: Weird and Wacky...
by Leland Gregory

Laughter Is the Best Medicine: Those...
by Reader's Digest Editors

Awkward Family Pet Photos
by Mike Bender

People of Walmart: Shop and Awe
by Andrew Kipple

How Not to Act Old: 185 Ways to Pass for...
by Pamela Redmond Satran

books made within 14 days of purchase from a Barnes & Noble Booksellers store or Barnes & Noble.com with the below exceptions:

A store credit for the purchase price will be issued (i) for purchases made by check less than 7 days prior to the date of return, (ii) when a gift receipt is presented within 60 days of purchase, (iii) for textbooks, or (iv) for products purchased at Barnes & Noble College bookstores that are listed for sale in the Barnes & Noble Booksellers inventory management system.

Opened music CDs/DVDs/audio books may not be returned, and can be exchanged only for the same title and only if defective. NOOKs purchased from other retailers or sellers are returnable only to the retailer or seller from which they are purchased, pursuant to such retailer's or seller's return policy. Magazines, newspapers, eBooks, digital downloads, and used books are not returnable or exchangeable. Defective NOOKs may be exchanged at the store in accordance with the applicable warranty.

Returns or exchanges will not be permitted (i) after 14 days or without receipt or (ii) for product not carried by Barnes & Noble or Barnes & Noble.com.

Policy on receipt may appear in two sections.

to me, mostly about their own dogs, which I didn't mind since I think those dogs are all dead.

Every day after that, I just wandered the halls and made people happy without having to do much. It was terrific. Until the day when I got back to Darla's room and Darla was gone.

I knew exactly what this meant. I'd been fired, which wasn't the end of the world because the world didn't end, and because it happened before. But now I have a new job. And I'm good. I guess it's mainly instinct, knowing who to visit and what to do. Some people want to play. Some want quiet time. And then there was the dying guy.

He was in a chair with wheels and hoses in his nose. I could smell something about him and it made me sad. So I sat with him the whole afternoon. Everyone thought it was strange. But the next day, the guy was no longer there and people started to understand what I was doing.

Since then that's happened, like, six times. I spend the whole day with someone special. And then they die that night. Just like that.

Um...it may be my imagination, but I don't think I'm as popular as I used to be. Like they're avoiding me. I don't know why. The last two old people I visited in the big room...they started to cry as soon as I walked up to them, and not in a good way.

That just means I have to try harder.

SARGE

My Pack

Willow

NuNu

Flea

Bit

Tinkerbell

I Hate Your Boyfriend
By Tinkerbell

Margo, this one's for you. You think I'm a great judge of men. Well, I did warn you about that guy with the noisy bike and the one with the fake hair and the one who had his spaniels stuffed and made into floor lamps. But I also drove away a nice doctor and a really rich guy in a suit. Let's be honest. I hate any man who could possibly distract you from "Tink World," including your last husband.

Okay, that may come as a shock. After all, I was the flower girl at your wedding. I cried—well, whined—throughout the whole ceremony. Every night I slept between you. But I was also the one who sprayed your sister's perfume on his pants and put that lipstick mark on his collar. (Don't ask me how.) From then on, it was just a matter of time.

This new guy hardly seemed a challenge. The first time you brought him home, I just ignored him and walked away. Then I sneaked up behind you on the couch and licked his neck. Maybe he thought it was you; I don't know. But he wound up licking you on the nose—then elsewhere. By the time he ran away, you had slapped the freak. I bit him. And once again, all was right in T-World.

But for some reason, you kept seeing him. I could smell him on you when you came home.

My worst fear was that maybe you guys got into the habit of licking each other, which is great when one of you is a dog but otherwise creepy. And then came the worst part. I'll see if I can say this without howling.

One day we were at the dog park alone, no dogs, just the way I like it. I was doing my business, right on top of someone else's business. But as soon as I unclenched and turned around, there it was, white and smart and fluffy, the nicest little Bichon in the world. He was all by himself too, no human in sight.

Before you could say "Jack Russell," we were in love—if you can call smelling body parts and biting ears and dry-humping love. Which I can. We played like this for my entire attention span, maybe longer. And when you tried to drag me away, I made a fool of myself. Crying. Begging. I had no shame.

Well, you know the rest. Just when I'm at my most desperate, your man friend comes walking out from behind a bush. "Frisky!" he says. And my Bichon pricks up his cute little ears, wags his tail, and goes running over. It had all been a setup. The two of you tricked me into liking someone. On neutral territory and without all the necessary information.

So…I don't know what to do. This is a horrible, horrible situation. And I still hate your boyfriend.

 Tails up

Things We Do When You're Gone

You've been wondering about this, I know. There was even a time when you put a little camera on a shelf, just to see what we would do when you left the house. Didn't work. All I can say is that we're very sorry and maybe, if you liked that camera so much, you shouldn't have put it inside a stuffed toy.

Since there are seven of us, you probably think we entertain ourselves all day long. You are absolutely right. It may look like we're whining and desperate and begging to go with you, but from the moment you close the door, it's all happy faces and party time.

First, we rearrange the furniture. No real reason. We just like the sofa in the middle and the small tables by the window. We put everything back in place before you get home, of course. Except sometimes we forget a detail, like your extra keys, or that thing you point at the TV, or that other thing you plug your phone into. Later, when you're walking around, muttering to yourself and trying to find these things—this is why.

Once the furniture is arranged, we start with the games. There's "Peeing on the Low-Hanging Towels" and "Licking the Fruit in the Fruit Bowl" and "Bite the Tail of the Donkey," which Buster doesn't like since he has the longest tail.

Oh, and then there's "Turning on Extra Lights around the House." This is always a little tricky, especially with no thumbs. But so worth it. When you come home and start arguing about which one of you left the lights on. Good times.

Okay, okay, none of this is true. We don't entertain ourselves. Whatever made you think we do? Seven dogs does not mean team sports. We just mope around and sleep all day. And wait for you to come home. That's why we're always so excited to see you. Not just because we love you. But because we're bored to death and you're our entertainment.

Charlie

The Human Words I Understand

You talk to me more than you talk to people, so you must think I understand. What else is the point? So this may come as a shock. I do not recognize most of the sounds you make, although I do know a few.

"Dinnertime"

That's an easy one. Food in the bowl. I learned that even before I was house-broken.

"Breakfast"

Also food in the bowl. Maybe it's a nickname for dinnertime, but I'm not sure. There's also "treat." It means food that's not in the bowl.

"Get down"

That's food on the countertop. Or food on the coffee table.

"Walk"

Also easy. When you only think about three or four things in your entire life, it's kind of a snap.

"Don't run off" and "Come back here"

It's like "walk," without the leash. I think the technical meaning is "go ahead and explore."

"Axelrod"

This was a biggie. For years, I used to just think of it as the sound you make when you're paying attention to me. But now I think it's actually my name, which is slightly different. I'm very proud of myself for learning this.

"Axel"

I have no idea.

"Good"

It's a sound of approval. I know because your voice is nice.

"Bad," "No," "Dammit," "Stop," "Hey"

All of them mean the same thing, whatever it is.

You make other sounds and maybe they have meanings too. "Sit." "Stay." "Shake hands." I try to judge by what you do, like holding out your hand (that's either sit, stay, or shake hands) or pushing down on my rump (either sit, stay, or shake hands). Also your tone of voice helps, like exactly how mad you sound. But really, it's just a guess.

I know you don't want to hear it, but I'm not as nice as you. I may lick you and snuggle, but underneath all this fur, I'm wild. I want meat. And I don't just want to eat it. I want to chase it and catch it and then eat it. Sort of like those free-range chickens, because they would be so much more fun to catch than the ones living in a cage.

I feel guilty about this. That's probably why I haven't figured out a way to kill the rabbit. First off, I don't know why you bought me a rabbit. But one day you came home and put on soothing music and spoke very calmly. Then you opened this little pen and let me look inside at this shivering ball of fluff. You learned pretty quick that bunny and me weren't going to be friends. That's why you built him a private cage beyond the fence, where I haven't been able to get to. Yet.

I know you want a world where a lion can lie down with a lamb. You even showed me a drawing, like this was somehow going to convince me. But it was only a drawing. And though I don't personally know these two animals, my guess is the only way you're going to see them lying down together is if the lamb is already inside the lion.

This doesn't stop you from trying to change me. Every morning, we do our sunrise yoga together. Unfortunately, the only pose I can do is downward-facing dog. After that, there's nothing left but to chew my mat and lick your face and, when your eyes are closed, catch a few of the morning butterflies. They're very slow at sunrise and very chewy.

Then come the herbal massage oils. They are soothing, but mainly because they have alcohol and I get a little buzz when I lick them off. An hour later, I have a headache and I'm even a little meaner than when we started. So you slather me with more herbs. This can go on all day until you finally need some alcohol too.

I guess deep down, I don't want to be like you. I wish I wanted it. It would be nice to be a pacifist. But that would make me different from almost every animal I know in the world. And that's just not natural.

☮ Moonbeam

WHY I CHASE CARS

You try to get me to stop. You keep me on the leash. You put that tall fence in front and keep the gate closed as much as you're mentally able. But apparently my mental skills are better, because I still get out and chase cars all the way down the road.

When I do, you scream and run after me. Or you drive after me—in a car, which just makes it more interesting. And you wonder, why do I do it? Or to be more precise…"Why, why, why, why, you idiot dog, you, why?" Let me explain. "WHY?" Give me a minute to think, okay?

I don't know.

It could be one of a number of reasons. Maybe I think it's a very fast cow and I want to kill and eat it. Or maybe I remember that a car killed Mirabel, my best friend from the park, and I want revenge. Maybe I think it's a sheep that needs herding, or a huge, odd-shaped ball that I have to go and bring back.

Honestly? My gut instinct is that this is a gut instinct. I'm probably not thinking at all. You should understand. We all have instincts we can't explain.

For example, every morning something makes you put on

those shoes and stand in front of the window and look out at the road and walk for an hour on a walking machine. That's no more logical than me chasing cars, and it's much more dangerous. I tried that machine once. Almost killed myself.

What would I do if I ever caught a car? I know you're thinking that too, and it's a fair question. I don't know. What would you do if you got to the end of that walking machine? It's not going to happen, is it? And I'm not going to catch that car.

Ooh, I thought of a couple more.

What makes you collect all the leaves and put them in bags when they fall from the trees? Or what makes you take all the snow from the walk and put it in piles? It's all an obsessive instinct. Who can explain it? Who can tell you why? Fools give you reasons. But that's because they're idiots.

S

I'm Getting Too Far Ahead

We all get older. I realized that long ago when I lost my puppy teeth. For a while I thought things would just keep getting better. I would keep getting bigger and stronger and learning new tricks until I knew as many as you. But I guess that's not how it works.

The strange part is that I'm now older than everyone. How did that happen? I remember like yesterday when you brought me home. I could sleep in your hand. Now I take up most of the couch. And sometimes you have to help me up. That's a far cry from when you used to swat me to get me off of it. Thank you, by the way.

But you haven't changed at all. You can still jump up on the bed and dig in the garden. Well, there was a point when your hair was turning gray, around the same time that my muzzle turned gray. But then your hair changed back to brown all of a sudden while my muzzle kept staying gray.

I don't know what I did wrong. I get my exercise and try to eat right. I even take my pills when you stick them in the middle of a treat or shove them down my throat. But even the cat is staying younger than me. And if that isn't wrong, I don't know what is.

It's like taking a walk together on the road behind the house. At first you led the way and I lagged behind on my little short legs trying to catch up. Before I knew it, I was at your side and we would do the walk together. Oh sure, sometimes we would go off on our own directions for a few minutes. But we would always yell out for each other and walk side by side until we got to the woods.

Now I'm in front, and I don't know how I got there. I turn around and you're always the same, like on the day we met. You're walking too and calling my name. But I'm getting farther and farther ahead. And I don't know how to change it.

I remember back to the puppy days, when you were walking far ahead. You used to stop and kneel down at the edge of the woods and smile and just wait for me to catch up. So I guess that's what I'll do.

When I get to the edge of the woods, I guess I'll just turn around and sit down and smile...and wait for you to catch up.

Sophie

The Questionnaire

What do you hate the most about yourself?
Drooling.

What is your guilty pleasure?
Chasing a flashlight beam. I pretend it's a spotlight and I'm performing on stage—with a really drunk spotlight guy.

Describe your perfect day.
Tree a raccoon with friends, hang out underfoot at Marge's Beauty Nook, then ride in the bed of a pickup and pretend it's a taxi.

What do you like most about people?
That they can be creative and famous and take part in pie-eating contests.

What do you do when no one is watching?
Put bottle caps on my feet and practice my tap dancing. But it hurts.

Who do you hate the most?
Anyone who laughs at my tap dancing. Laughing, I figured out, can be good or bad. But combined with my tap dancing, it's always bad.

What makes you howl the most?
I don't howl. I sing—anything but country.

What do you value most in a dog friend?
The ability to do harmony.

Where would you like to live?
In any town, like maybe Radio City, that has a big, fancy theater. Or maybe a circus, where I can travel and have my picture on a poster—high up so no one can pee on it.

What do you like most about your human family?
They're fine. I like Toby 'cause we bonded when I was tiny. We always wind up doing stuff that he likes, except sometimes his sister takes me to piano lessons. My favorite is any music by this guy Grrr Schwin.

What is your biggest regret?
That I never got to be one of those puppy actors in the window of a pet store. I would have been great.

How would you like to die?
Die? What's die? I don't know what that means.

Rufus T.

A Family Photo

It used to be easy. Two humans and a dog—you in your good-smelling clothes, me in a furry hat and white beard—sitting in front of a roaring fire. You fiddled with the camera and we all smiled big and in a flash, it was over.

Today? Not so easy. If you didn't already notice, my boys like to chew, especially things tied to their faces, like funny white beards. Okay, try to separate them. That's good. Everybody smile! No, wait. Runt is puking up beard. And Mutt Junior is eating it and...oh yum, that's tasty. You guys should try this.

No more beards and hats. Much better. All you have to do now is touch the camera and come back. No, Runt, stay with us. Don't follow...all right, bring Runt back here. Hurry. And smile. Don't worry if Mutt Junior is throwing up Runt's throw-up of the beard. You barely notice. But it smells good, doesn't it? Let me smell. I won't taste.

FLASH! How was that? Good picture?

Okay, cosmic question: How do you go to the camera and not have a puppy follow you? And not knock over the camera? Then there's the other puppy. And when it comes down to it, I'm a puppy at heart. Just hold on to us this time. Hold tight and stop yelling. FLASH! Don't yell. I'm sure you took a lovely picture, but if you want to try again...

Good. I'm glad you took the time to change your clothes, because the vomit was distracting. Now we're calm again, and the boys are on leashes. That's one way to keep them from wandering off. Runt and Mutt Junior, no! Don't pull. Augh. Why did you tie them to the fireplace screen? What made you think that was smart?

Okay, no beards, no hats, no fireplace. The new clothes don't even smell of smoke. And if you hold me over the burn mark on the rug, no one will see. Just don't hold Mutt Junior up to the side of your face like that. He'll think you're snarling at him. Then when the flash goes off...FLASH!

Is it walk time yet? I'm just wondering because Runt is lifting his leg on you, and he's pretty good about saving that for walk time. How about dinnertime? I'm just wondering because the sun's going down. And try to keep that side of your face turned away from the camera. It's starting to get puffy.

Dimples

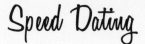

Speed Dating

Usually we just walk around the block, sometimes to the park. But every now and then, it's special. That's when we turn a different direction and walk more. I just wish you'd let me know ahead of time, so I could lick myself a little cleaner or rehearse some cleverer things to say.

This special place is almost like the park but more exclusive. You have to pass through two gates to get in, and it's only for dogs accompanied by humans. Then they let you off the leash and the fun begins.

Ooooh, so many boys, so little time. You barely get a chance to say hello, then it's on to the next. And you have to be careful because sometimes you can smell a cute dog for a full minute before figuring out it's a girl. What a waste!

Some of the boys look great from a distance. You both wave your tails. Then he comes over and you realize that he was farther away than you thought and he's just very big. I don't like big dogs. They're hard to reach. And they all walk around with their rears in the air, like they're somehow better than you.

I don't like slobbery boys either. I know it looks tasty. But once that stuff gets on you, it's a sure invitation to a bath. Same goes for the guys who drag their ears through the mud. And the old ones with bad hips who still play with Frisbees and make like they're so young. UGH!

Some boys pretend the game doesn't exist. They hang out with their pals and play sports with a ball or chase each other. Show-offs. You can tell because they always have an eye focused your way and hold their tummies in and growl all macho. Sometimes a few girls will play with them. But that just barks of desperation, don't you think?

Some boys are shy. They'll barely sniff you then get all standoffish by standing off in a corner—or worse, between their human's legs. These are the losers. I bet they spend a lot of time in the family basements, sleeping alone and looking at old SPCA catalogues.

But every now and then, you'll meet a great guy. He won't be too big or shed too much. And you'll find lots to talk about, like squirrels and you. And you'll pretend to be interested in cars and bicycles, even though you're not. It's all great.

Until the next girl walks through the gate. Then he runs off all excited to sniff her without even stopping to check the phone number on your collar. Dog-faced jerk!

♡ Gabby

SARGE TO THE RESCUE

I worked so hard at the hospital until I got fired. It happens. Carlos, the guy in white, was my best friend there, and he took me home.

Carlos has a nice house. It's all set up for a dog, with a cushion bed and a big backyard. He even has a wall covered with pictures of me. Except it's not me, since they show me and Carlos smiling and holding up ribbons and big cups, and I have no memory of that. Honest. Sometimes he forgets my name and he accidentally calls me Caesar, usually at the same time that he's crying. I'm guessing that Caesar was his old dog, but I don't mind.

Like me, Caesar was a worker. I don't know what he did, but it involved all the stuff in the backyard. There are ladders and bars to jump over and things to crawl under. Carlos started training me right off, the same day I got there.

I'm a very quick learner. But it seems kind of useless, all the running and jumping and crawling. Why? For awhile I think it's play. But Carlos doesn't treat it like play. He makes me do it over and over as fast as I can. I'm even better than Caesar, probably. And all the while I'm thinking, what's the point?

So, today is the big day. Up early. Packing the car (Carlos did most of the packing). Driving for hours (again, Carlos). When we finally get to the scene, there's this open field, set up with exactly the same stuff as our backyard. I sit patiently by the side and watch a whole bunch of other dogs. Some are fast, some are slow, some knock down the fences. Still I don't get it. But all too soon it's my turn and I'm nervous. There's got to be something more to this, right?

I start out like the others—through the poles, going up and down the seesaw. Carlos keeps up with me, shouting and pointing to the next thing, as if I don't know. And then I see it. None of the other dogs see it, but I do. There's this van rocking back and forth, just a little ways off the course, and these weird, human sounds coming from inside. Aha, that's what it is. Of course. Rescue.

The whole operation happens fast, sort of a blur of shouting people—and a few barks. When I pull open the van door, there's this man and woman inside, attacking each other on a mattress. Well, not attacking. More like wrestling. And they really don't want to be rescued. But everyone does come and rescue these two, thanks to me.

It's been a long day and Carlos and me are driving back. He's not saying much. He doesn't have to. It's enough to know that I finally figured out my job and did it.

SARGE

The circle of Life

I guess we should've seen the signs. First, old Duke starts smelling different and you let him sleep on your bed. He used to love that, but now he doesn't care. And there's all the attention he gets, plus treats with the pills stuffed inside. He gets a lot of those. Then he goes for a trip in the car and doesn't come back.

Next thing you know, everyone is sad. At first just the people. But then us. We can't help it, even if we don't know what's up. It's kind of a downer because we prefer being happy. For a while there are no organized sports, just a lot of hugging and petting and soft voices.

But that's not the worst. The worst, the thing we should have seen coming, is the puppy—although you can hardly call it that. It doesn't even have that new dog smell. But it's a lot more puppy than anyone in the house, so I guess it wins. You carry it inside and everyone coos like a pigeon, and you give it Duke's old bed, like it's supposed to take Duke's place. I was even afraid you were going to call it Duke. But you call it Duchess, which is different, so I guess you're better than I give you credit for.

Can you blame us for being jealous? I mean, the rest of us worked hard. We trained you to be good with the water and the food. And, of course, we all owe a special debt to Jake, who risked his life on that hunger strike until they started adding table scraps to the bowls. Thanks, Jake! But now here's this new-comer who gets everything and more and does nothing, except maybe try to control her bladder, but not very well.

It's going to take a lot to sabotage this baby. You even let her spend the night on your bed when her whimpering got too loud and her face got too cute. She snuggled between you until the middle of the night when little Chloe snuck up there and left a nice little puddle. No one woke up, not until the puddle got cold.

That put an end to the puppy's bed privileges. But we're all going to have to stay vigilant.

Charlie

It's Just a Stomach Ache

Y̲ou could say it was my fault. And you'd be wrong. Okay, maybe it was partly my fault that I ate something I wasn't supposed to. But it looked very chewy and smelled good. I knew at the time this would give me a tummy ache. But I knew I'd get over it.

The trouble began when you saw me vomiting. There was some weird stuff in the vomit I guess. You got worried and you wanted to cure me. Well, starting with a tummy massage was not the way to go. All that did was make me jerk my leg around, even after you stopped rubbing. So now I had a tummy ache—and what looked like a leg spasm.

It wasn't a real spasm, but when I tried to run away, you wouldn't listen. You went right to your recipe book and mixed together all sorts of herbs, even though there was no spasm and the vomiting was over. Then you spread the herbs all over my tongue. It stung like the kiss of a porcupine.

This time I did manage to run. By the time you dragged me out from under the porch, I was biting my tongue like crazy to get rid of the sting. You realized that I was in even more pain now. Thank you. So, of course, the next step was to stick needles in my rump. Why was that the natural next step? I don't know. Apparently it was.

I've seen you put needles like these in your friends. I figured, how much could it hurt? But after six long needles and a lot of chanting and pinging at the needles so they vibrate...This must be one way that dogs are different from people, because it hurt like another porcupine.

So now I'm under the porch again, pulling out the needles with my teeth. I didn't realize we were only halfway done.

After that came the massage oil that spilled right into the holes from the needles. Porcupine number three! Then came the mud bath, which you would think would be fun but I wasn't in the mood. And the hot stone massage, which no creature in its right mind would think is fun.

I was within an inch or two of passing out—from the tummy-ache, the vomiting, the spasm, the tongue herbs, the needles, the oils, the mud, the hot stones. And then I saw you looking around for the tarot cards, and I thought, "Great! It's about time. This will put an end to the whole mess. She won't be able to find her tarot cards and it'll be over. Finally."

Because that's what I ate at the very beginning. I ate your tarot cards.

☮ Moonbeam

I'M STILL HORNY

Here's an old joke. And yes, we like jokes, especially the practical ones. "Why does a dog lick himself?" Because he can, right? Wrong. Because I can't. Because there's nothing to lick. Okay, not much of a joke. That's my point.

Not that I'm blaming you. You left me at the vet and when I woke up, my favorite balls were gone. I don't know what happened. I looked everywhere, even on other dogs. A lot of them were also looking, by the way. Balls seem very easy to lose.

At first I pretended nothing was wrong. "Oh, those balls?" I said when a bitch would ask. "I must have left them with my other collar." But deep down, I missed them. The way they used to flop around. The way everyone sniffed them. The way they tasted like a salty snack that you carry around with you just in case. Mmmm.

For a while after I lost them, I was calmer. Not really calmer. Depressed—and maybe not as bossy. I even gave up humping your leg. And humping the stuffed bear in the playroom. And humping the toilet brush. And humping your other leg. Without the humping, I was a mess, although you didn't seem to mind.

Then one day I was doing some gardening—transplanting a bush, I think—when something rubbed up against my belly. I rubbed back. Then I thought about the Maltese down the block and how she always smells so different in the spring and fall. Then I thought about her brother. And the neighbor's rabbit, which is odd, but he smells so terrific.

Just a few minutes ago, you caught me rubbing against the potted cactus on the porch. You thought it was hilarious. "Hey, look at Bandana. He thinks he's a stud." And that's when I saw your legs again—right leg, left leg, they both looked great. Like old times.

So if you didn't know before, you know now. I'm still horny. Maybe I'm even growing new ones, somewhere inside where they won't get lost. As for dragging the cactus over and humping your leg and the cactus at the same time…It's what we call a joke. If you'd stuck around instead of running off screaming, you would have known.

I Like Those Buzzy Collars

I know it's not normal for a dog to like those boxes on your collar that sting and keep you from running away from home. But I love those things. Even though I've never actually had one.

It was during the warm time, when a dog spends his day outside, just digging and digging under the fence. (You know, if you guys put a fence in the middle of the yard, then I could dig under and just walk back around whenever I want.)

So, that day I am just out in the world, wandering on my own. When I get to the house on the corner, I see Bruiser, who is always barking at the window until someone yells "Bruiser" a whole lot and maybe he stops. This time Bruiser is on the lawn, barking loud 'cause he sees me. He runs over to say hello and kill me. But then he stops before his grass even ends. This thing on his collar, you see, is buzzing and making him whine and snarl at the same time.

So, we're there, just talking like dogs do. "I'm going to bite your head off." "Oh, yeah? Come here and say that." But he won't come here. And it's funny. And I laugh. And he jumps at me and yelps in pain. But he's out on the street now and I'm running away, 'cause I'm bored.

A little while later, I'm walking by his house again on my way home. I see Bruiser out there pacing by the street, wanting to go back onto his grass. And his collar's buzzing again and he's whining. Until he sees me. Then he's barking and ready to kill again.

Even I can figure out what to do now, and I'm no poodle in the brains department. I walk calmly onto his grass and he can't follow me. Until he gets real excited. Then he follows me and yelps in pain. And then I walk OFF his grass. And he can't follow me again. Until he gets excited. And then I walk ON his grass.

It's a good game and I'm sad when it gets dark and someone comes and yells "Bruiser" over and over until he goes back in the house. Then I go back and dig under my fence again, just in time for dinner.

The next time I see Bruiser, he's got an even bigger box on his collar and it's even more fun.

AXELROD

City Dog, Country Dog

I don't quite know how, but all of a sudden Burnside is the most famous dog around. One day he's this ordinary water dog who couldn't smell a corpse if you put it in front of him. The next day he comes back from the city with a blue ribbon and everyone's calling him by some long, stupid name, like Valley's Prince Burnside Eat-A-Biscuit. Something like that.

I couldn't figure it. Why was he going to the city and getting famous when he probably didn't want that stuff half as much as me? So, I thought I might wander over to his place and have a chat. Maybe get a few pointers.

When I got to Burnside's place, he wasn't in the yard. But there was this fancy van parked there. A good dog smell was coming from inside the van, a great dog smell, and I just had to see for myself. That turned out to be easy. Any dog that can figure out

how to tap-dance a time step can certainly open the door to a van.

At first glance, I thought it was Burnside in there—same curly black hair and white feet. But it certainly didn't smell like Burnside. Her name, she said, was Maggie. She had come all the way from the city to see Burnside, even though they only met once before.

Burnside and her had been in the city performing in

some big show for dogs. Performing? Right away I was jealous. Burnside had never been interested in show business. The most he ever did was prance around the yard in a big circle on a leash, which you cannot even begin to call dancing.

I liked hearing Maggie talk. There were so many things I needed to know. "What does the city smell like?" for instance. She said there were hundreds of smells every-where you turn. But you're not outside much, just a couple times around the block, whatever a block is. And then there's always a leash and someone tug-ging you away from the best stuff.

I asked her about grass. A big city must have dozens of different

grasses. But she said there was very little grass at all. "And you must have the most interesting and clever raccoons. Right?" But she had never even heard of a raccoon. "What about the show you did with Burnside? That must have been a thrill." But she said it was just very big and confusing and made her nervous.

In a strange way, I guess talking with her made me feel better about my life. And I walked away that day thinking maybe my world wasn't so bad after all.

I still think about Maggie a lot. I heard later from Burnside that the humans put them together. But he swears they didn't have sex. That's probably because she already had sex with me in the van—before we got to talking.

Rufus T.

S

Life Is a Little Blurry

Dogs don't like to show weakness. It's how we are. We show you a lot of other things, like our fear of thunder and vacuum cleaners and bug zappers. Those are scary sounds, and we can't help it. But weakness is something we hide.

Remember that time? I was meditating out back, kind of aimlessly chasing my tail, and I fell off the deck into those prickly bushes. After you stopped laughing, you thought I was hurt. But I got up and ran away and pretended I was fine, like nothing happened. Well, it did happen, and I was biting thorns out of my fur for days.

It must be an instinct left over from the old days. Just in case a predator, like a wolf or a monster, happens to be prowling nearby, we don't want to look like the weakest link in the food chain. "Yoo-hoo, I'm healthy. Go after something easier."

I guess this is why I'm hiding my bad eyes. You probably didn't notice. When I sit in the corner for hours and stare into the wall, it's not because I'm feeling antisocial or punishing myself for something you haven't found out. It's just that, by the time I realize it's not really a door, I don't feel like getting up and moving.

You know how I'm so excited every time I see the neighbor lady on the street? I do like her, I'm not denying that. And she's always so happy that I'm looking happy and wagging my tail at her. But the truth is from a distance her handbag looks like a poodle on a leash. It gets me every time. And then I figure out it's just a handbag, and I'm embarrassed. So I just keep wagging the tail, not to disappoint her.

Maybe I should let you know what's going on, instead of hiding it. I know you're not a wolf or a monster or a bug zapper. I just don't want you to think less of me after all these years.

Sophie

Setting Boundaries

Let me tell you about my puppies. Setting boundaries is important with them. Establish boundaries and stick to them. So here's a list of your boundaries.

Don't step in their mess. "Bad human! I am so disappointed in you!" And if you do make a mistake, try not to track it out of the house. Or into the house. Don't track it anywhere. It sets a bad example.

Speaking of in and out...please figure out what's inside and what's not. The boys get confused. Does inside mean anything with walls? How about the carport? That seems to be okay? How about the porch? Yes? No? How about packages left on the porch? How about the baby's room? If there's any place that smells like outside, it's the baby's room. How about the side of a picnic basket—sitting outside in the middle of the lawn? How could this be bad?

Decide what you mean when you call our names. Is it good, bad, or nothing? When you say, "Dimples, Dimples," do you mean, "I see you, cutie pie," or "Stop that right now"? And don't say, "It depends on the way I say it." If your words don't have meanings, you might as well grunt.

Don't go "coo-coo-coo" and bite them on the nose unless you want them to bite you on the nose. Fair is fair. Also, don't snip off their testicles.

Please stop playing hide-and-seek with them in the woods. Do you seriously want the puppies to feel abandoned? Mutt Junior had nightmares after that, and Runt still thinks you hate him.

And this brings us to the big boundary, otherwise called fences. Are they supposed to keep us inside, like the wooden fence around the yard, or are we supposed to jump over them, like the wooden tree that fell across the road?

I remember when we were taking a walk and Runt refused to jump over that tree. He thought he was being good, until you started laughing and coaxing. Then he jumped and fell and tumbled over. And you laughed more. Poor Runt may be scarred, scarred for life—unless he stops picking at that little scab. Then it'll get better.

I LIKE THE COSTUMES

It doesn't happen very often, just around the time when the little balls are falling off the tree in front of our building—you know, the ones that are all spiny and rough and you yell at me not to eat them, but who cares? And once I get past the spiny outsides, they're tasty. [Editor's note: chestnuts.]

That's about the time you go start sewing and pasting and laughing together and putting clothes on me. "Oh, Orson, we're sorry. You're going to be so embarrassed. See how embarrassed he is?" But that doesn't stop you, and you laugh some more.

Well, I'm not embarrassed. I love it. One time you dressed me like a woman in a hat with fake arms holding fake flowers. And one time it was this grass skirt with real flowers around my neck. Okay, but not delicious. And one time it was a really big costume with wrinkles and everybody laughed a lot. [Editor's note: Jabba the Hutt.]

Then comes the best part. You get dressed up too—looking better than you normally do, I might add—and we all go for a long walk with bags. People on the street also dress up, with more bags. Everybody pets me. And if I'm quick, I can steal something nice out of their bags. Again, once I get past the paper outsides... tasty. When they catch me doing it, they laugh, which is not how people normally act when I steal food.

Next we visit houses. We go up to the door and people in regular clothes come out and give us stuff for "later." That's a concept I don't quite understand. But at least I don't have to play dead or shake hands.

Sometimes you stay and talk to them. That gives me a chance to stick my nose into your bag, or, should I say, our bag. But sometimes, only one of you talks. The other one sneaks off to the side and joins me at the bag. It's what I call a real bonding moment, as long as you don't touch the Lorna Doones.

This year, my clothes are very special. We worked for ages. I don't want to give it away, but as far as I can tell, it has a tail and five legs and dots and a big, big hat that flashes on and off. [Editor's note: not a clue.]

Orson

MY HOMELESS LIFE

How did I get on the streets? It's the age-old story. Bad luck, unemployment, an unhappy home situation. Then one day they take you for a ride and kick you out by the side of the road.

At first I didn't mind. The air wasn't cold, and I could usually sniff out a meal that wasn't covered in little worms. But there wasn't much to do, and I fell into some bad habits. I would sleep sixteen hours in a row when fourteen would have been fine. I was always on the run from the law. And I made some shifty acquaintances, including a raccoon who shall remain nameless...because no one ever named him.

The worst part was the loneliness. When you look like me and you start chasing after people, trying to be friends...well, they don't often stop and ask you to shake hands. Except Tommy Boy. Tommy Boy didn't run, partly because he was unsteady on his feet and kept falling over. Tommy Boy knew I was different from the moment he shouted "stop" in this scared, loud voice and I stopped and sat down and waited for his next command. We became friends. I wound up following him everywhere, which was usually just to the liquor store and back. But at night I would sit by his side while he leaned up against a building and played his old ratty guitar.

It was nice listening to him play and sing. Other people on the street listened to him, and one or two dropped pieces of paper into his hat. Tommy Boy liked that. I could see him eyeing the paper and smiling and hoping.

And then one time I tried to help. A woman took out a piece of paper for him but then looked like she might be changing her mind. So I helped. I went over and gently took the paper in my teeth, then walked slowly over and dropped it in Tommy Boy's hat. The woman was surprised. She laughed. And he laughed even harder. And suddenly Tommy Boy and me were partners.

It's been great ever since. Tons of people come up to us on the street. It doesn't matter how bad Tommy Boy plays. Or how much he smells. People hold out the paper and I take it and trot over and drop it in his hat. Everyone has a good time. Grown-ups give their kids pieces of paper, just to see me take it in my mouth and drop it.

It's a very good life, Tommy Boy and me, and I want it to go on forever. It probably won't.

SARGE

The Art of the Growl

By now you probably know. Everybody growls. Even Snowball, who is small and boring and easy to ignore. Snowball growls under her breath. I know it sounds like an apology or a phlegm ball, but it's a growl, like Buster when he wants to take off a cat's head.

Sure, not all growls are the same. Buster specializes in the scary attack thing. He'll put his ears forward and curl his lips and growl deep with his mouth almost closed. Sometimes this is mean. And sometimes he's just playing his ventriloquist joke with Snowball. We play along. "Look, Snowball is angry. Ooh, we're scared." Cracks us up.

Jake practices a big growl too. It's lower and tougher than his regular voice. But that's just insecurity. He also likes to pee last, which is pretty annoying when I try to pee last, and then he tries to pee laster. And then I have to do it again. It's very sad, him being so insecure.

Chloe growls because she doesn't like anyone. And she's lazy. Somewhere she must have heard that it takes fewer muscles to growl than bark. Plus, she's figured out how to growl and also eat. She's good at doing both together, except now and then when some food accidentally goes down her growl pipe. Then she vomits.

Duchess the puppy does it for fun. Puppies do

everything for fun. It's annoying. You can ask them, "Why are you chasing your tail?" or "Why are you playing hide-and-seek with yourself in the mirror?" and they'll just say, "It's for fun, silly," or "What's a mirror?"

Miley has started growling more. That's because she's in her wolf phase these days and wolves don't bark. Have you noticed? So Miley does her howling and growling and the rest of us put up with it—like her Pilates phase, when the only thing she would eat was the Pilates ball.

And me? I think of it as another form of communication. I growl when I'm tired of barking. Or when I want to emphasize certain points, like, "Dinner!" or "I'm saving this spot next to me on the couch for my invisible friend," or "The house is on fire."

So, that's about it. The whole growling thing, totally explained. Or to put it another way...grr, grr, grr. GR-R-R-R-R.

Charlie

My Favorite Toys

The first time I saw a stuffed toy, I freaked out. How dumb was that! But you made me freak. You put it on the floor and wiggled it and made noises. I totally thought it was real. So I barked and I stalked it and I ran behind the couch. I must have done that for hours and hours—or like you sometimes call them, minutes. And after all those hours, when I realized it didn't have a smell...was I embarrassed! You won't fool me like that again.

I guess that was my very first toy. Teddy Bear. Or like you used to call him, Leo.

Toys were a new thing for me. Of course, everything was new. Since then, I've gotten to know a whole lot of toys, some good, some bad.

Let me just say first, to get it out of the way, balloons are not toys. Shoes, yes. Balloons, no. They're like flying bombs. I don't care how much cake there is, I'm not coming anywhere near a balloon.

Things with squeaks are always good, and eyes and tails and stuffing. Balls are fine, if I'm in the mood. Things with rope, not so much. They're too much like exercise. If I just want to pull on something, I'll grab your shoelaces or the scarf around your neck.

Mechanical toys are okay once. But after I get that they're not real, they're just annoying, like a joke you keep telling. Rubbery is fine. But I have to say, the rubber chicken doesn't look anything like a chicken. And I don't get the toys that make you laugh at me. Like the squeeze toy that sounds like a fart every time I bite it. Why is that funny?

I guess my favorite new toy would have to be Ethan. You brought him home just yesterday, and for a while it was like you'd pulled another Leo on me. You held him close to the floor and made his arms move and said things like, "Hey, Gabby. My name is Ethan. I'm your new brother," in a high voice. But it was clearly a human baby doll. You could tell by how it squeaked when I gave it a little lick. It squeaked for hours. And I mean human-style hours. Maybe days.

♡ Gabby

Why I Hate Dogs

It's embarrassing, I know. Here you are, this sweet woman with a rainbow painted on your dress. And here I am on the other end of the leash, snarling and ready to mangle any dog that comes within a block of us. Sure, part of it is the leash. It lets me lunge without any downside. But most of it is the fact that I don't like other dogs. Sorry.

"Why is this?" you ask. You really do. You ask everyone. "Why does my sweet Moonbeam hate every dog in the world?" And everyone has an answer. Your personal trainer says I don't get enough exercise, but he says that about you too. Your therapist says that I'm having a flashback to the same kind of dog that must have attacked me as a puppy. Really? You think I was attacked by poodles and Chihuahuas and Yorkies and long-haired cats?

Your sister says that I'm a naturally aggressive breed. And when you point out that I'm not a breed at all, she changes her tune. Then she says it's because I wasn't properly socialized. What does that even mean? Were you properly socialized? Huh? Were you? Not with that sister, you weren't.

Your life coach sees how nice and loving I am with people, and he has a theory. He says I'm a people dog, not a dog dog. Okay. But I don't understand how that brilliant insight helps. Of course, I don't understand half the stuff he says. It's like he's talking another language—not human, not dog, not in the least way helpful.

The vet says that you're a member of my pack and that I'm trying to protect you. Bingo! This is the true reason. Well, it's pretty close to true—except that it's exactly the opposite. I'm not protecting you. I'm protecting me.

Here are the facts. You don't have to believe me, I'm only the dog. But from my experience, there are only so many dog-loving people. Every day there are more and more dogs and only so many people to take them. That's reality. And it puts me in competition with every single mutt I see. "Stay away. This is my human. You can't have her. I don't care how fluffy and cute you are, she's mine."

Anyway, that's my reason. And it must be working, because we're still together.

☮ Moonbeam

You Act Guilty Too

You always know when I do something bad. Maybe it's the way I act. The way I hang my head and can't look you in the eye and put my tail between my legs. Last time I did this, you got mad and started racing around, talking in this deep voice and looking for chewed curtains or vomit in the magazine rack. I just sat there politely on the rug until you gave up. Then you became very nice to me and apologized. Like you should.

You were almost ready to give me a treat, until I got up and wagged my tail and came over to you—which was a mistake, because at that point, you saw the part of the rug that I accidentally peed on. And now there was pee on my butt too.

My point is...I can't help looking guilty now and then. That doesn't mean I'm guilty. Maybe yes. But maybe no. Maybe I'm in a mellow mood and want to put my tail between my legs for no reason.

You know, sometimes you have the very same look, except for the tail. Like when we're out walking and I poop on a thorn bush. Then you check around in all directions and walk away so fast. You don't even stop to save my poop and put it in that special can on the corner. Hey, I don't care if you save my poop or not. But you had that guilty look.

Oh, and how about the time you were blowing the leaves from our front yard onto Bernie's yard? Remember? Same look. Or that neighbor lady who everyone hates. Remember when she came by and asked something about Miranda? And Miranda was right there hiding behind the door and didn't even come out to say hello. You were both having that look. And for no reason.

You see? Everyone acts a little guilty from time to time. Doesn't mean I did anything.

So the next time I whine and hang my head and try to avoid you, don't jump to conclusions. I could be not guilty. There could be a perfectly not guilty explanation for my behavior, although I can't think of one at the moment. But there could be.

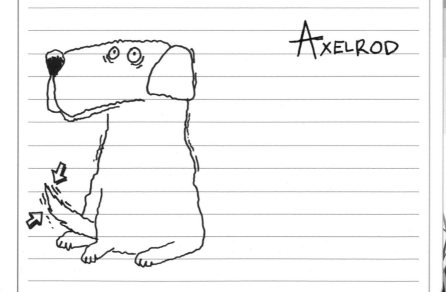

Axelrod

I'M JUST ASKING

Sometimes it feels like we're growing apart.

I don't know how to explain. Little things. Like you used to get me toys, something every week. I still take care of them all, herding them together and putting them in the box. But when the toy box got full, you stopped getting me new ones. Just like that. And you used to experiment with treats, giving me weird stuff and seeing if I like it. Yes or no, it was fun. Now you just give me the stuff I like.

So I ask myself, "What went wrong? What can I do to put the magic back in our relationship?" Maybe if I understood you better. Do you mind if I ask questions? Things that seem mysterious to me but probably make perfect sense.

First, there's the alarm by your bed that always goes off. It must annoy you too, because you moan and get up and moan and turn it off. So, why don't you fix it? You manage to stop it every morning. But maybe you need an expert to come and fix it for good.

After our first walk, you sit down and stare for a long time at this paper you retrieved from the porch. Does this paper help you pee? I'm asking because it's the same kind of paper you used to put down in the kitchen for me. Looking at that paper was supposed to help me pee, so I'm assuming it's the same for you. I could be wrong.

You leave the house a lot without me. I have no idea where you go. All I can guess is that you're going to the park again or walking around the block or to some parking lot where you roll down the windows a bit then disappear for a while. You really should take me along. I'm not doing anything while you're gone. Nothing important.

I get very measured meals at very specific times. You and the kids eat whenever you want to. Why is that, exactly?

When you put that little box up to your ear and talk, are you talking to me? Because sometimes we're the only two around. So are you talking to me or to the box? Is the box alive?

Right before you go to bed, you check the bed alarm again. You really should take the opportunity to fix it before the next day comes around. Why don't you?

Bandana

SAY HELLO TO MY LITTLE FRIENDS

I'm not quite sure what fleeze is. It's either something good or bad—probably bad, now that I think of it. I remember the moment you started saying it. I was lying between you on the sofa, meditating on these itches tromping around on my tummy and scratching them with my teeth.

Next thing I know, I'm all turned over and you're rubbing me. Yes! You even found the spot. Except this time it was more a kind of picking than rubbing and both of you were doing it. Then came the screaming, which was okay because you were screaming at each other. As soon as the collar came off, I knew we were doing a bath, which was weird since it was morning and I wasn't even smelly.

I do like baths, except for the water. I like the attention and the massage and the games, like "Eat the Soap" and "Don't Eat the Loofah." I know, they sound similar, but the rules are almost the opposite.

But this bath was different. For one, the massage was very hard and you used a lot of soap that wasn't worth eating. You could tell because I threw up, something I almost never do with food.

So we were all in the tub, stepping around the throw-up, which was like a new game for me—although I've seen you play it. Usually late at night in front of the toilet. Anyway, I was still throwing up and trying to shake off the soap because it was starting to sting. And I guess some of it got into your eyes.

Now the game got interesting. Suddenly everyone wanted their faces under the water, not just me, and there was new screaming—well, kind of a screaming gurgle. Two sets of screaming gurgles—and maybe some barks. At some point, I lost interest and got out of the tub and dried myself on your bed.

So maybe that's what fleeze is, kind of a bad bath game. But everything worked out, and we all took in plenty of treats. Of course, as soon as you put the collar back on, the moving itches came back, since that's where they like to hide.

This time I'll try not to let you know. Not that it wasn't fun.

Orson

My Experience with Tricks

Some dogs don't like tricks. Maybe they feel it takes too much time out of their day. Me, I didn't care, not until Toby's sister saw this show on TV. Then she got all excited and took me outside and taught me tricks, like crawling on my belly or pretending to be shot.

I must have been good too, because Melody goes right out and gets all sorts of balls and ladders and planks, even some real dog treats with pictures of professional dogs on the box. You can call it training. I called it rehearsing. And I loved it.

For a little girl, Melody was a pro, teaching me all the best stunts. And then we tried dancing. I know it was dancing on account of the music and the footwork and the jazz hands. Melody called them jazz hands, but it's more like shaking your paws back and forth.

I must have missed five hunting trips that month, limping around, pretending to be sick in front of Toby, then racing off to rehearse. I could tell that Melody was getting ready for something big. And I was right. We were going to perform in front of everyone. It was some kind of show at the school. This school is by far the biggest building in town and animals are never allowed inside—except me. Take that, Burnside. You just do dog shows. I do theater.

144

I'm not sure what kind of show it was supposed to be, except bad. I watched from the side as these people from town did terrible songs or terrible jokes. Then everyone clapped except me. I refused. I didn't even do jazz hands.

Now it was our turn. Melody put this red jacket on me and one white, sparkly glove on my paw. Then the music started. I was supposed to be this human who turns into a wolf or a zombie or something. (She showed me the video, like, fifty times, but I never got it straight.) A second later, we were on stage.

What a rush. Like smelling my first skunk, only good. Melody danced with me. It was supposed to be scary and I howled on cue. The people in the dark loved it. They were all clapping and shouting. And all I could think was, "This is it. This is what I was meant for." Then maybe I got enthusiastic.

I mean, I was supposed to be this dancing zombie. So I felt I should be really scary. So, before I knew, I was jumping off the stage and really scaring people. I was very good at it.

Anyway, I don't like this town anymore. They don't understand art or artists or stuff like that. All they understand is calling the police and animal control and then putting you in a cage for a week to see if you have a disease.

Rufus T.

Cats vs. Dogs

Sophie's housemate, Hannibal, has joined her for a rational debate.

Happy to See You

SOPHIE: "It doesn't matter how long the trip is. You could take a three-month vacation or just walk out to the mailbox. A dog is ecstatic—and kind of proud—at your decision to come back. My tail can't wag fast enough."

HANNIBAL: "At least a cat can tell the difference between minutes and weeks. And do you really want a creature who loves so easily? How real can this love be, especially since humans do nothing to earn it? But if you're that insecure, fine. You know, it doesn't matter if a dog's nose is brown or black: they're all brownnosers."

Walks vs. No Walks

HANNIBAL: "Cats rarely bother you with daily maintenance. We bathe ourselves and deal with our own poop—basically. Well, sometimes the box is a mess, but at least we don't make you walk behind us in public with a bag."

SOPHIE: "A walk gets you out of the house, even on those days when you'd rather act like some crazy shut-in with a bunch of cats. That's right. I said it. You never hear of a crazy shut-in with a bunch of dogs. Rarely."

Cats are Easier

HANNIBAL: "With dogs, there are things like leashes and winter coats and dog beds. And don't forget obedience school. Plus time. All the days you wasted trying to train Sophie to do the simplest things that a cat would never do, so don't even ask.

"Not to mention the dog-sitter. I know you don't bring her in for me. I would be just as happy using the litter box and entertaining myself with sunbeams and eating a little bit of the food in my bowl every day."

SOPHIE: "Just about every word of that is wrong. Of course you wouldn't take a cat to obedience school. What's the point? And what kind of animal eats just a little bit of his food every day? A crazy, cat-loving shut-in's cat maybe.

"Goldfish are even easier. That doesn't make it right."

Sophie & Hannibal

IT'S A TOUGH BUSINESS

So, my new boss is named Scotty. I know, I know. Like the dog. Scotty came to see my act when Tommy Boy and me were on the street. That night, Scotty and Tommy Boy had a couple of beers, and I showed Scotty all my tricks. Before I knew it, Tommy Boy was holding a whole bunch of his favorite paper, and Scotty was taking me away with a rope around my neck. Strange world.

A few days later, I started my new job. It's hard to explain. Most of the time we're in this huge building. There's a whole lot of people and lights and machines. No one does much of anything except move the lights and machines around. But then someone shouts "action" and things happen for a minute.

There was a special man there. Troy. Everyone liked him. He had nice hair and a smile, and it was my job to be his dog, at least for a minute at a time. Most of it was easy—walking at his side, lying down, licking his hand. But there was this one day...

On this one day, Troy was dressed like a cop. I've known a lot of cops, and Troy wasn't very good, but that's just my opinion. They had taught me how to pretend to have a broken leg. That was hard. Then they put me far away and told me to crawl up to Troy in his uniform. Meanwhile, Troy is yelling at me. "Go away, Murphy. Save yourself. Go."

I don't know who to listen to. And my name isn't Murphy. And to add to the mess, all these bullets start flying around, making noise. Am I supposed to keep crawling, I wonder, or maybe stop crawling or maybe go back? Why don't I just attack the guys behind the wall who are shooting the bullets? I did that a few times, but no one liked it.

Anyway, it was a very long day, and everyone got grumpy.

At the end, I was all alone, just wandering the lot. Even Scotty was ignoring me in favor of a beer. And then I passed by a fancy trailer and smelled an old familiar whiff. Very familiar. I jumped inside the trailer, like an instinct. And there was Troy. I think it surprised him when I came right up and grabbed the marijuana off the table and ran out the trailer door.

Life is confusing. Work is confusing. But when it gets bad, I think back to my days as a drug-sniffing dog. It was my very first job, and I was pretty good. So I ran around the lot until I found a real cop, just like the old days. Then I put the pot right down on the ground in front of him. I didn't even take a bite, I was so good.

And still I got fired.

SARGE

We All Want to Escape

According to Buster, who heard it from Duke, you guys started out with just one dog. And when good old Duke kept escaping, you thought it was because he was lonely. So you got old Duke a friend. And when both of them kept escaping, you thought...Anyway, now you're up to seven, and the yard is full of toys, but every time we're out in back, we're checking that fence like prisoners in some maximum-security kennel.

I'm guessing you feel bad about this. Or at least annoyed. Or maybe just curious. "Why are our dogs so desperate to run away from home?" Well, if it's any consolation, each one of us jumps the fence for a different reason.

Take Buster. Turns out he's sensitive about the weather. So when it's too cold or too hot or there's rain coming, he jumps from the garbage can up to the fence and tries to run someplace warmer or cooler or to run far ahead where it hasn't rained yet. Sometimes he'll do this even when he could just as easily go back in the house. I know. Not the sharpest tooth in the mouth.

Miley digs because she likes to dig. She's always surprised when she comes up and, wow, she's suddenly outside in the back alley. This makes her so confused that she wanders over to the neighbor's fence and digs a hole into their yard.

Chloe does it to be alone. Frankly, she hates us. You can

usually find her with the blind lady down the street, pretending to be a stray cat. Meanwhile, Duchess the puppy is
out there looking for someone her own age. Her new best friends
are a family of mice puppies in a nest in the park.

Jake runs away for the attention, ever since he was gone for
two days and you put up all those posters of him, like he was
a movie star. There's nothing he loves more than being recog-
nized on the street and chased. And ever since Tom the mailman
started giving out treats, little Snowball likes to track him down
around the neighborhood. That's why when you come home,
sometimes Snowball is sleeping inside the mailbox. In case you
were wondering.

Me? I do it for the challenge, to see if I can make it past your
newest try at security. But I don't run off. I come right around to the
front and scratch. Then you open the door and shake your head
and call me Hairy Houdini. Because I'm hairy, right? Pretty funny.

Charlie

I Love My Fetch

You know how important Fetch is. It was the first toy you ever gave me. Remember how you used to say its name and throw it far? And then one day it stopped squeaking. I kept squeezing and squeezing but nothing happened. You went right out and got me another one, but it wasn't the same. It looked almost right. But I like my squeaky Fetch. I kept biting it and whining. Finally you put a new squeak inside and my old toy was as good as new.

Then somehow we lost it. I don't know where. It was horrible. We looked and looked. In the toy box and under the bed and outside and in the toy box and under the bed and in the toy box...but it was gone. Again you tried a different one. You even took me to that big place where I like to scare the hamsters and parakeets and you let me pick it out. But I wasn't interested. It was Fetch or nothing. I even went off my food for a few minutes, it was so bad. And then I checked the toy box and under the bed...

Then out of the blue last week, Miranda is taking me on this nice long walk. She thinks we're going a new way, but I know I've been this way before. Some nights we'll go down this street, just you and me. It's very familiar.

I'm getting excited now; I'm not sure why. And I start pulling Miranda toward this one particular house. Oh, that's right. It's Puddy's house. And there's little Puddy in the front yard. He sees me and wags his tail and goes straight for his pile of toys. And then comes that wonderful sound I never thought I'd hear again. Squeak, squeak!

Miranda recognizes it too. It's Fetch, as big as life, just sitting in the yard. Puddy brings it over to Miranda for a little tug, and Miranda can see it's indeed the real Fetch because it has all the earmarks (the marks I made on its ears), plus the red stitches on the tummy where you put in the new squeak.

This is where we left it, of course! A couple of times on our late night walks, you brought Fetch along for fun. Puddy and I would play in the yard while you talked and talked with Puddy's person, a nice woman who smells very nice. Miranda was looking confused to find Fetch here, but then the nice-smelling woman came out of the house and Miranda stopped being confused and started being something else.

So everything is fine. Better than fine. I have Fetch. And there's 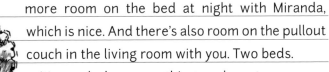 more room on the bed at night with Miranda, which is nice. And there's also room on the pullout couch in the living room with you. Two beds.

It's good when everything works out.

SQUEAK!

AXELROD

You're Not in My Pack

I should have known when you sat down with that book. It's never good, you and a book. Life was fine until then. At least I'd gotten used to it, the vegan diet and herbal remedies. Now all of a sudden, you're my pack leader.

A pack? Come on. I hate other dogs. The closest I ever got to a pack was me and two rabbits on top of a car during the flood. And Fluffy was not the leader. She was just the grumpiest. Sure, I once carried a pack. It was during our wilderness hiking phase. But I think that was a different thing entirely and just happens to have the same sound, like human roof and dog ruff.

But there's no arguing with you, even when you start barking and growling like we're having an argument. That, it turns out, was page one from the book. The next page had you drinking from my private bowl. Did you know that a human's mouth is dirtier than a dog's? I don't know where I heard it, but it's true.

Then there's you lying down on my dog bed. That's crossing a boundary. Plus, I'm afraid to say, you have dandruff. I saw it in your hair this morning when you were trying to snuggle. It's like the old saying, "Lie down with people, get up with dandruff and a whiff of herbal deodorant."

The worst part is all the running. What makes you think I love running? Did I ever pretend to love running? Walking, sniffing, exploring... those I get. Those have a purpose. But now every morning in the dark, you hop on your bike and drag me for miles up Canyon Road, barking and pretending to be my leader. When we finally stop, the torture isn't through. No, we have to sit and howl at the sunrise together, even though I'm totally out of breath.

I'd like to point out here that I'm not a wolf. Maybe I don't want to live in a group in a cave chatting about where our next meal is coming from. Maybe I'm not a pack player. Not all dogs are the same. That's like saying all humans are crazy and insecure. I don't think that's true.

I can't prove it, but I don't think so.

me

Myself

AND i

☮ Moonbeam

157

The Bed Rules

Now that the boys are big enough to jump on the bed, it's time to set some rules. Rule number one? It's my bed. Yes, yes, it's your bed too. But let's get back to the important stuff. It's my bed.

Personally, I'd love to keep the boys off. But you're a soft touch, so that's not going to happen. The most we can hope is that everyone understands rule two. I get the middle pillow. This way I can smell you and you can smell me. And we get to play our favorite nighttime game, "Who's Snoring?" Usually it's me, but it takes you a while to figure this out.

Mutt Junior gets the spot just below me, halfway down. He has a favorite game too, "Who's Farting?" but that's harder for you guys to figure out. Little Runt winds up at your feet. He likes to move in the middle of the night, going from foot to foot to foot. Runt doesn't have a game, unless it's waking you with his jangly collar.

There are exceptions to these positions. For example, when one of you gets up, then we all switch. I take your place, Mutt Junior takes my place, and Runt jangles his collar some more. We all jangle. I would maybe suggest taking off our collars at bedtime, but it doesn't bother me, so I won't.

A few minutes later, when you come back from the bathroom, we all have to move back. Not willingly. We pretend to be asleep, even though we got up and moved just a minute ago. Have you ever thought about sleeping at the foot of the bed yourself? You should try it.

Now and then you break the rules. Like the time Runt was sick. You put him in my place and snuggled all night. Under the covers. I never get under the covers. That was hard to take, and I wound up jumping off and crawling under the bed, just to teach you a lesson.

It's not a perfect system. I don't always get the best sleep. (I need my full sixteen hours.) But I guess it's worth it, just for the warmth and comfort. Although you should really think about doing the foot of the bed. Runt says it's great.

Dimples

We Know All About You

We're late. Hurry up. Why is it that I can tell time perfectly well and you don't seem to be able to? No, you don't need a sweater. If we don't go now, we'll miss everything. That's right, leash on. Down the steps. I know we always turn right, but it's late. Go left. We can catch up with them at the next corner.

It may not be important to you. But why do you think we all drag our people out at the same time every single night? It's no coincidence. I know certain dogs—no names—who pretend to have problems "down there" just so they can stick to this exact schedule.

Tree number four? Hmm, no trace of Good Girl Misha. Not a shocker. I could tell from yesterday it was becoming that time of year for her. Oh, and speaking of heat, her human is in a similar condition. A little similar. She's pregnant. Very early days, from the scent. No one seems to know it yet. Not the man. And not even the woman, because yesterday, according to Good Girl Misha, she bought these really skinny pants that she can barely fit into.

Yes! Cut through the alley. Smell that? Axelrod. Or Axelrod No, which I think is his new name. He never has any news. Clueless.

But we did find out that his man is sleeping on the couch at home. You know what that means? Me, neither, but I don't think it's good.

You spend hours talking about us. Right? And yes, dogs are more fascinating. But we love spending a few minutes each day catching up on you. Like Sweetie Sweetie's old human guy. Poor man is getting forgetful. Last week he forgot to put down water for a whole day and Sweetie Sweetie had to drink beer from a broken bottle on the floor.

We always find out who's going on vacation, and who sits around all day in his slippers and stopped bringing home the quality dog food. Which kids are home for the summer? We know. Which humans didn't put the lid down tight on their garbage? Easy. We can smell it on our breath.

Look, there they are, on the corner by the park. Axelrod and Sweetie Sweetie and Roger and Come Back Here I Mean It. We're not too late. Good. Because I can't wait to tell them my news about you.

♡ Gabby

Sniff
Sniff
Sniff

STOP TRICKING ME

We're adults here, right? We respect each other and have something of a bond. So tell me, why do you keep trying to fool me? You have all these tricks you use to get me to do things.

Let's talk bath time. You're not fooling anyone. It starts with smelling my fur and making faces. That goes on for days. Then you sneak the plastic mat into the tub and open the shampoo drawer. Before you can even get my collar off, I'm under the bed. Last time you tried to lure me out by yelling, "Bandana, there's a treat in the bathtub!" A treat in the bathtub? Really? That's the best you can do?

How about your trick of hiding little pills in my food? You never try to pull this trick when I'm in top condition. No, you wait until a day when I'm not feeling well. And still it never works. If I can spit out the peas from your beef stew, I can certainly eat around a pill in my bowl.

I can go on and on. Like when you pretend we're going for a nice drive, and we're really going to the kennel. Or that time you said we were going out to play in the snow. Then you slipped and fell, and suddenly I'm sitting by your side in the cold, whining, until some truck with flashing lights comes and picks you up. And what happened to the rest of the snow play, huh? I'm still waiting.

Your sneaky tactics have even managed to taint one of the pure pleasures of life. When I was small, dog treats were these unselfish gifts between friends. Pure magic. Now every time you give me a treat, I'm suspicious. "Is this a trap? Is she trying to put me into a crate or cut a knot out of my fur?" Do you really want me to look sideways and grab every treat out of your hand like it's some kind of edible bomb? Is that how you want me to behave?

I am never tricky with you, am I? Never. (By the way, when we're on a walk and I pretend to be sniffing a tree while I'm really trying to finish a chicken bone? That's not tricky. That's common sense.)

We just need to start being honest with each other, that's all. Let me know what you want me to do. Then maybe I'll do it. Maybe I won't.

Bandana

Me and the Vet

"**W**ant to go to the vet, Sophie?" No, not really. Why don't you go without me if it's so much fun? Do you ever go without me? I have no way of knowing, but I'm thinking not. This is what I know about the vet. It's a building where they bring all sorts of dogs and the big plastic purses that smell like cats.

After some random hellos and sitting down, you make me stand on a rubber mat. For years I didn't mind the mat, but then maybe you noticed that I got more skittish. That's when I figured out this is a scale used to measure weight. And that you were actually yelling my weight across the room and talking about how I put on a few extra pounds since last time. I don't think I need to say anything more about the scale.

Then you take me into this room I really could do without. Part of the problem is the table—a cold, slippery one that you make me stand up on. Finally the man comes in and pretends to be my friend. He sticks me with needles. He pokes me and my butt. And all the while, he's saying what a good girl I am. "Yes, thank you. I know I'm a good girl. Stop it."

The vet never used to bother me. It's not scary like the car wash, or wonderful like a dropped ball of ice cream on a hot sidewalk. But you're taking me to this vet more and more, so I've been giving it some thought.

Lately we only seem to go there when I'm feeling bad and just want to lie in a corner. Have you noticed? And I always come back feeling worse. Maybe a day or two later, I might feel better, but what good does that do me? I'm all about now. Anyway, who can remember what I was feeling two days ago? So why don't we just stay home from now on?

Oh, one time I did feel better when I left—when I had that twig stuck sideways in my mouth. Wow, that hurt. And it hurt even more when the man pulled it out. But then it felt better, so maybe he's not so bad.

Sophie

My Pack

Willow

NuNu

Flea

Bit

Tinkerbell

The Smelly Cat
By Tinkerbell

Let's settle one thing before I start. Your fault, Margo, sweetie. Agreed?

If you hadn't chased me around trying to give me a bath, then I wouldn't have crawled under the house. If I hadn't crawled under the house, then I wouldn't have run into that cat, and we wouldn't have blah, blah…giving away your clothes and moving into a hotel.

Most of the fault was the cat's. It was a huge, beady-eyed monster staring out of the gloom right under the kitchen. It hissed at me, and I hissed back. Then it got all very huffy and raised its big, stripy tail. I raised my tail. What I didn't realize at the time was that this was a farting contest. And the cat won.

In two seconds, I was racing out into the yard screaming. Up until then, the worst thing I ever smelled was the Christmas issue of *Vogue* when I chewed up all the perfume pages. But this…I went screaming right past you into the house, looking for anything I could find to rub up against—the new curtains, the new rug, the other new rug, the new couch, the other new couch. I even rubbed up against a few old things, that's how bad it was.

By the time the maid caught me, I'd rubbed my way through your bedroom closet twice, and I still stank. And then came the Bloody Mary bath. Honestly? I don't know why you filled the bathtub with Bloody Mary mix. You must have used half the supply in the house, and I still didn't smell any better. Plus, I was counting on a little buzz from the alcohol, but no. Consuela forgot to add it.

By the time you sniffed me and wrinkled your nose and gave me another Bloody Mary bath—Consuela, please, the vodka?—I was in the worst mood possible. I had done all this to avoid a water bath, and I wind up looking just like a guinea pig at a Peruvian barbecue. [Editor's note: small liberties were taken with this description.]

Before you could dry me off and even think about a third bath, I escaped the only way I knew—back outside and under the house, where apparently there lives a whole family of these hissing, tail-raising cats who were not at all happy to see me again. Then some more screaming, back into the house, et cetera…

Anyway, the sooner we forget all this, the better. Right? Your clothes are going to make some poor people very

happy, and the house will be fumigated. And this hotel is great. It also serves these killer Bloody Marys—with plenty of vodka.

Tails up

MY BIGGEST JOB YET

All my life, I've been a working dog, which doesn't always mean things pan out. In fact, they never pan out. But I gotta tell you, this new job is the hardest ever, mainly because I can't figure out what it is.

After I was let go by my last employer, I wound up at a homeless shelter. It was nice enough. You sit around in a cage and every now and then someone comes by to interview you.

Eventually I got hired. I don't know their names yet, so I'll call them the Bosses. When I get a new job, there's almost always some training. But this time...if there was any training, I wasn't paying attention.

At first I thought I was there to be a child herder. Honestly, I never knew anyone who had that job, but for several days, all I did was run around the backyard, trying to get a bunch of screaming kids organized.

Then I figured I must be a walker—you know, take the people on long walks to the park or around the block. But on some days we don't walk at all and I just roam around the yard, which isn't much of a job. So that's not it.

Sometimes I think I'm supposed to be the guard dog. But it's a pretty safe neighborhood, nothing like the yard of junk I used to patrol. Or maybe a lifeguard, except everyone here can swim, even the baby.

Sometimes I'm like an entertainer, like in the old days with Tommy Boy. They'll surprise me with something–throwing out a bent stick that flies in a circle and comes right back to them; that was frustrating. Or putting a dog yummy on the other side of a glass table. Then they all laugh and take videos.

I don't even know who has the power to fire me. Who is the head boss in this company? Sometimes it seems to be the man, sometimes the woman, but mostly it's the baby, although I can't imagine her firing me.

It's been a problem, not knowing. Not knowing what your job is can make you sick. Really. It made me sick. That was a scary time. But they took me to the vet and didn't fire me or dock me my treats. In fact, they were even nicer to me until I stopped worrying so much and got better. Then they were normal.

I really need to find out what this job is. Because I like it.

SARGE

Other Things I Don't Understand

Why do so many things have water in them? Dog bowls and the sky and those pipes in the lawn? Also the plastic guns you shoot at me when I bark too much.

Why do squirrels like to sleep in the middle of the road?

How many times do I have to say "I want to go out" before you take me seriously?

Why is it sometimes warmer inside and sometimes cooler inside?

Why is it okay for you to pee in the house? Also, why is it okay for me to pee against a tree, but not for your brother when he drinks too much beer?

Why does everything smell? You don't seem to mind, but it drives me bonkers. Especially dead things. You would think they wouldn't be able to make a smell anymore, being so dead, but they do.

We both spend a lot of time staring at stuff—like the box in the living room or the box on your desk or, in my case, the wall. I do it because I'm bored, but you seem to like it. Shouldn't we be doing something more constructive with our free time, like throwing the ball and fetching the ball for a few hours?

Why is it okay for you to keep food for later, but when I try to keep a few extra bones buried in the sofa, it's a crime?

Why does the scary thunder only happen when it's raining, so that when you try to run away from the thunder, you always get wet?

Maybe I shouldn't be asking you all this. I should probably ask Thor. He's the Great Dane from next door. We have these cool moments when he's digging into my yard and I'm digging into his and we meet in the middle. Then we switch yards.

Anyway, Thor knows things. He even wound up getting his master's degree. We think it was a degree. It was hanging on his master's wall and smelled like a sheep, so he ate it.

AXELROD

My New Best Friend

I didn't really plan on it, but I guess I was running away. All I know is one day I'm walking down the lane and I keep walking. It felt exciting somehow, like an adventure. Maybe I'd run into a carnival where I could join them and dress up like a clown. I might have done it too, but there was this little duck.

I had no idea where he came from, but he kept following me. I tried to speed up and lose him. But he'd fly and waddle and keep following. Then I tried sitting in the middle of the lane, barking. But he just stood right there, unscared, wagging his little tail. So I turned around and went home.

By the time we got back, the duck and me was buddies, in that kind of wordless way we do things. No one even knew I'd been gone, except I was being followed by a duck. Toby laughed and chased the duck away, but he didn't go far. The poor thing just dug a little nest under the porch and waited for me to come out again.

Every day we snuck off and played, sometimes duck games, like napping in the shade and swimming. And sometimes dog games, like napping in the sun and swimming after a ball. And in between, he ate and ate. I can't tell you how much he loved the cat food our neighbor puts out.

Looking back on it, we are totally alike. Two outsiders, ignored and left alone. I could imagine us, after he put on a few more pounds and feathers, running off again, but together. Maybe a circus this time, not just a carnival.

And then one day, Toby's dad paints all the duck decoys in the garage and puts them out to dry. After he leaves, Duck and me are having fun with them, sitting still and pretending we're decoys. Or pretending that the decoys are real. He spent a lot of time pretending the fake ducks was real. It was funny until it started getting sad.

The next morning, Duck wasn't anywhere. Not under the porch, not at the cat food, not with the decoys—I checked carefully. I guess a part of me was glad to see him gone.

A day or so later, all the ducks started flying south. It was hunting season. Normally, that's a slow time for me, since the other dogs are better retrievers. But this year, I kept busy. I got up super-early, before the hunters, and went to all the best nesting places on the lake. Then I ran around like a mad dog, howling until every flock had taken off.

For some reason, this was a very bad year for duck hunting.

Rufus T.

It Was the Possum, Not Me

It all started with a word. I remember that night, after Bill took the food from under the sink and went outside. He came back and was saying it over and over. "Possum, possum." The two of you must have said it back and forth about six hundred times.

And then the next night...the seven of us were in the yard, barking at clouds and celebrating the moon. I was doing my usual checks, making sure the lids were on the garbage. They were, damn it. And no food wrappers in the Jeep. Damn. And then I came around to the compost.

Someone—and I'm not placing blame—had left off the compost lid. Well, one thing led to another, and I didn't even hear it when he called my name. The next thing I knew, Bill was coming around the corner and almost caught me with my snout in the absolutely best-smelling stuff since you guys buried the gerbil.

Lucky for me, my nose is the same color as compost, so he wasn't too suspicious. "Charlie, what are you up to?" The only thing I could think to do was bark. And it worked. I happened to be facing the little hole on the side of the garage—the hole that Miley dug a week ago—and I did some furious barking. Bill went over to look. And that's when he said it again. "Possum." It was like magic. Bill even petted my head and said I was good.

Possum, we figured out, is this wild animal, and it may

be nearly as destructive and selfish as Miley, although I'd personally never seen one.

For the next week, life was heaven. Somehow this possum gave us the freedom to do anything. We would pretend to chase it constantly. No one stopped us. No one blamed us, either, for the knocked-over garbage or for tearing up the seats in the Jeep, or for digging those holes in the garden.

And then one night, I saw it.

Bill was just calling us in when I saw this shape moving alongside the garage. No one else was looking, but I was after it instantly, no thinking involved. Which is normal.

When Bill caught up with me, I was at the compost. This time, it was totally knocked over. But I wasn't going after the food, honest. It was the possum. The possum was somewhere in there and...

"This isn't what it looks like," I wanted to say. But there would have been translation problems and I didn't even try. And it's hard to trust a dog caught red-pawed with a snout full of compost.

At least that's been my experience.

Charlie

How to Stop the Digging

I know you're upset with Runt and Mutt Junior right now. They've been digging holes and you don't know what to do. The first thing you need to do is to stop thinking of digging as bad. That will solve most of your problem right there. In fact, it will solve all of your problem. But I can tell this isn't the answer you're looking for.

Maybe we all need to calm down and ask ourselves, "Why do these little angels dig in the first place? And how much damage can eight tiny paws do? And shouldn't we look at the positive aspects of digging? It's kind of their first hobby."

From experience, I can tell you that digging relieves stress. And let's face it, having two active puppies causes a lot of stress, so it's no wonder my guys dig. I'm surprised you aren't digging holes yourself. Oh, wait a minute, you are. Don't deny it. I think it sends a mixed message for you to dig in the garden and bury things like plants and cow poop. But then somehow you expect my boys not to follow your lead and dig them up and eat them and barf them up.

Digging is also hours of innocent fun, a game

that doesn't need a person or a ball. And it helps improve memory. "Did I put the bone here or here? Is this where I buried the wallet, or is this where I buried the mouse?"

But this doesn't answer your question, does it? I believe the question was, "How can I let the puppies dig and dig without them feeling guilty?" And the answer is simple. Give them a project, something constructive. Maybe their digging can help you put in a pool. Or a fish pond. This way, the boys can shovel to their hearts' content without being yelled at. And after that, they can swim. Or they can play with the fish and bury them in other parts of the backyard.

Of course, it doesn't have to be a pool or pond. They could dig any water feature. Or a row of cooling holes by the bushes where we can all lie down in the hot weather and feel the cold, fresh dirt under our bellies. I think you'd really love that.

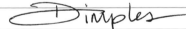

Why Do I Lick You?

May I start by saying just how delicious your face is? Taste it yourself if you don't believe me. It's this wild combination of deodorant and body spray and sweat. A lot of sweat. More sweat than anything, actually. I love licking you. Plus it helps get the taste of toilet rim out of my mouth.

There are other reasons why I lick you too, not just taste. Love, of course. Why not?

And grooming. It really helps tone down that shiny look around your nose. And your blackheads are much better. You remember how my mom used to groom me when I was teeny tiny? Same thing. Of course, my eyes were closed back then, so I had an excuse for not doing my own grooming.

Speaking of my mom, I used to lick her too. Did you notice? How I used to stick my tongue into her mouth and lick like crazy? I was trying to get her to throw up. You know how it is at that age, always hungry.

You may have also noticed that I lick you even more when other animals are around. Can't help it. Humans, other dogs, even mosquitoes. I guess this is my way of showing off. "Look, this human person is mine. She likes me best and I like her best, and I'm bonding with her whether she likes it or not."

Okay, maybe I do lick too much. I think I got the hint this morning when I was trying to wake you up and you were trying to hold my mouth shut. I was only doing it because I love you. I love you! And you were salty, and I had to go outside and pee. And I was bored. I lick a lot when I'm bored and can't think of anything else.

Here's a good question. Why do you pet me so much? I bet you never thought that one through, huh? Sure, sometimes I like it. But sometimes it's just annoying.

Well, I lick you for the same reason, whatever that is.

♡ Gabby

YOU NEARLY STARVED ME

I blame it on that one morning with the indoor tree and the wrapped-up boxes. You opened up most of them yourselves. But one of the boxes you said was mine. You were both very excited—in that fake way that's supposed to get me excited. You even let me open it. It was full of these little metal outlines. Fire hydrants and dog bone shapes. I couldn't eat them, and they didn't squeak, and I didn't get the point.

The box disappeared for a while. Then one day you were in the kitchen, and the room smelled vaguely of food. This, by itself, was odd. The kitchen never smells, not until my dinnertime, or until the man delivers those warm food boxes. The little metal outlines were on the counter now, all lined up. And you were fake-excited for me again, which should have been a warning.

The oven was on, which usually means you're warming up pizza. Not this time. Other things were happening too. There were containers of flour and eggs and milk and rolled oats and cheese and garlic powder... [Editor's note: Orson may not know Christmas but he knows food.]...and bananas and bouillon cubes.

Both of you were in there, bumping each other between the oven and the fridge and the gadgets, so I stayed out of the way. You also had this sheet of paper you kept looking at and arguing about. Then came the smoke and the burning.

It's hard to describe the next few hours. But I've had my share of nightmares and this seemed like one of them. Good things went into the oven and black things came out, smelling like the charcoal you put in the hibachi. These went right into the garbage and then more good things went in, followed by another fight.

Now it was well past dinnertime and all the fake-excitement was gone. Did I mention it was past dinnertime? I tried barking and whimpering, but no one was in the mood, until all the black things were finally thrown away. Then one of you put on her coat and banged out the front door. And then the other one banged out the front door too. And it was still past dinnertime.

I don't know when you got home that night. Late. Meanwhile, I had to fend for myself and make do with the garbage full of tiny black fire hydrants that tasted like hot charcoal. My mouth was burned, and my stomach ached, and I literally couldn't eat for hours, so...

Please, no more trees and wrapped boxes. They only lead to trouble.

Orson

Frequently Asked Questions

"WHO'S A GOOD DOG?"

I'm a good dog. I'm a good dog. I'm a good dog. I'm a good dog. I'm a good dog. Tired of it yet? Then you know how I feel.

"WHO'S THE PRETTY GIRL?"

Like the above—only I guess you're playing to my vanity here. I'm the pretty girl, thank you. Although, I suppose if I was being polite, I would have to say, "You are. YOU'RE the pretty girl. Not me, you. Yes, you are. You're the pretty girl."

"WHERE'S THE BALL?"

It's in your hand. It's still in your hand. What are you, an idiot? Still there. Oh, now it's on the lawn. No, I am not going to fetch the ball. Look, if you're honestly so excited about the ball and getting it back, then why the hell did you throw it away?

"WANT TO GO FOR A RIDE IN THE CAR?"

Yes. I do want to go for a ride. But I'm going to need a little more information. For example, will you be in this car with me? And where is this car going? Is it going to the vet? Or to your astrologer? In that case, I'll take a pass. Or is it going to the dog park? Or up in the hills for a nice long walk? Or is it just going on a bunch of errands where I'll be sitting in the backseat, barking at fifty people through a crack in the window?

"WHO WANTS A TREAT?"

Is this a trick question? Because it's kind of a no-brainer. Like, "who wants happiness?" My answer in both cases is, "Of course I want it. Who doesn't? But at what cost? Do I have to beg? Or get into that cage again? Or get back on the leash? Or can I get it without doing anything? Because that's the way I want it."

"WHO DO YOU LOVE THE MOST?"

You. You're my absolute favorite, even though you're apparently so insecure that you have to ask me over and over again. I love you. Okay? Now can I have that treat?

☮ Moonbeam

My Pack

 Willow

 NuNu

Flea

 Bit

Tinkerbell

I'm Not a Guard Dog
By Tinkerbell

I know what Brianna's friends say. "Oh, Tink is the best guard dog in the world, the way she barks and growls and tries to bite my finger. See how she's going for my…? Ow, ow, ow. Bad Tink!" But the truth is, I'm not that vicious. I just hate her friends.

Other people I'm fine with. Ask the gardener. I know there's this rule where he's not supposed to be in the house. But on those times when you leave me home—you know, when you're not carrying me around, flinging me everywhere like some kind of accessory…Like when I'm in your purse right next to your sparkly phone, and it vibrates and rings—which is loud—and then you reach in and almost pull my head off…where was I? Right. The gardener.

Well, whenever you leave and the maid's not there, he comes inside. The first time this happened, I barked and snapped. It's a habit. But when he opened a bottle of wine and poured some into my bowl, he didn't seem so bad.

Nowadays, we just lap up the vino and snuggle on the couch, the one I'm not allowed on. Then we scratch ourselves and watch our stories. The only time I growl is when I hear the gate opening again for your Mercedes. But that's more of a warning and he understands.

I'm surprised you're not suspicious. Yes, you did notice the missing wine, which you blamed on Brianna and she blamed on you. And the TV is sometimes tuned to Telemundo. But you blame that on the maid, even though it only happens on her day off and she speaks in a language no one understands, not even the pool guy.

I guess what I'm saying is, you should start using the alarm. Not that the gardener with the good taste in wine is going to take anything. But if a burglar happens to show up one day with maybe a tempting leg of lamb or a friendly poodle...

You are not paying me to be a guard. I'm not interested in being a guard. And if you think you can just assume that I'm going to take on that responsibility, well, go ahead. It's not my house.

⌒ Tails up

MY TIME IN THE PEN

I don't know what I did wrong. What could have been so serious to make you send me away? Was it chasing the guy in the fast wheelchair? Honestly, it looked like a car. Or maybe on the playground, when I kept all the kids inside the jungle gym until they started crying? A herding instinct. Blame nature.

I knew it was a prison from the minute we drove up—the high, wire fences, the yard, the warning barks from the other inmates. They may give it a harmless name like "Coral Rock Pet Boarding," but to me it will always be "The Rock."

Right away the guards slapped me into solitary. Everyone was in solitary. The only relief was a couple hours a day when they let me use the exercise yard. This was where I hatched the escape plot.

It wasn't hard to find some others to join me. Most of them had no idea why they were there. Some had been in and out of the system for years. Everyone I talked to there hated the screws—the ones in the bottom of the cages. They hurt. And no one could stand the chow. Not the chow-poodle mix, but the pure chow. He had shifty eyes.

My plan was simple. Dig a tunnel behind the water pipes, under the fence, and into the woods. From there, we would change our collars and try to find new families. I had everyone working in shifts. There were the big diggers. Then the lookouts–small, tough guys who kept an eye on the guards. And then the medium-sized dirt-eaters who ate all the dug-up dirt so no one would know.

Our escape was all set for the night of the full moon. That night, we all got together and howled for a while, maybe an hour. Just for fun. Then, one by one, we slipped into the hole and scrambled our way through–little dogs first, then bigger and bigger until finally it was just Ajax, the Great Dane.

Ajax had a tough time of it. But he was determined. He kept digging and pushing the last plastic water pipe out of the way. And then came the snap–and all the water. And the sirens. And the blackout. And the screaming night guard. And you know the rest.

At least I can say I'm the one who closed down that prison for good. Or until they fix everything that went wrong. But I don't think I'll be going back there anytime soon. No sirree. No one wants that.

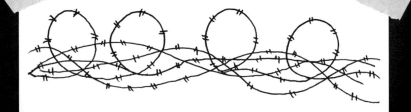

MY DAY AT THE CLUB

You used to feel guilty about leaving me. Both of you would come home and I'd be there at the door, so happy to see you and jumping all over—as much as I could, given my luck with gravity. Some of it was that I'd been so bored and lonely all day. But some of it was that you brought home groceries and it was almost dinnertime.

So now, not every single day, you take me to this dog club where I hang out with other guys in my situation. Most of it is this big room with unreal grass and prechewed furniture and you can do your dooty inside, and someone cleans it up and doesn't yell.

Most of us play with toys or each other, but I tend to do exactly what I do at home, being what you might call an observer of life. Every day, the people join us for this big playtime. That's when they try to get me to touch a ball or walk across the room. It's a big room, did I say that? And then they take us on a field trip, or a sidewalk trip, depending on which way they turn when we walk out the front door.

The other members are pretty nice. We used to have a couple of bullies, Marco and Polo. They were brothers and got in the habit of biting tails. Everyone was afraid of them until, one day, they followed a rawhide bone into a closet. Somehow the door got shut, and I wound up sleeping in front of it. It was a long day. After that, their owners stopped bringing them to club meetings.

For a while, I was friends with Sophie, the old cocker spaniel. She would spend all day sitting by the front window, waiting for her human to come back. Poor thing. I know she was sad because when they gave her a treat, she wouldn't eat; she just sat there and looked at it. So I would hang out and keep her company. Then one day, she started feeling better and got her appetite back, so I don't hang out with her anymore.

All in all, I like the club. Good smells. A lot to observe. I just wish Sophie would get back to her old self again.

Orson

MY WEEKEND JOB

It's been two years now and I haven't been fired. I just thought I'd say that up front. I was worried for a while, since I couldn't for the life of me figure out what my job was. But now I know. It's part-time work, two or three days a week.

It starts out with my commute. The Boss family drives me way out to a pretty "weekend house" in the middle of the woods. As soon as we get close, I start moaning and whining. And it's not because I'm happy. It's moaning and whining. Does that sound happy? No, it's very stressful.

When they open the car door, I get to work. First, I run around the whole property, barking and sniffing, making sure the place is free of wild animals. Sometimes I can smell them on the grass, which makes me crazy. I tell you, whoever has my job during the other five days is not doing his work.

Then I go around for a second time, marking the boundaries with my smell. After that, I take inventory. Are all the toys still there? Are the bones still buried in the same spots? The booby trap holes I dig every week to trap chipmunks and trip up deer?

Sometimes they're still there, but sometimes they're covered up, which means I have to dig new ones.

These chores I keep repeating, as often as it occurs to me. Then there's gardening. I split the gardening into three categories. Do I chew it? Do I chase it? Do I pee on it? And then I go chew it or chase it or pee on it. Oh, and the stone steps that go through the garden. My job is to poop right in the middle of a step. But sometimes I miss and hit a rose bush, which is not nice on the old pooper.

Just last weekend, the Bosses had a pool party. It was all fun and games for them. But did they realize that there was another dog half a mile away? Did they notice that the wind changed direction fifteen times? Or that a big family of bunnies was thinking of crossing the lawn before I stopped them? I didn't think so.

By the time we finally drive away, I'm totally exhausted. Ah, the curse of being a working dog.

SARGE

The Big Fancy Collar

Once, I hated wearing a collar. Then I got used to it. It makes a tinkly noise so I always know where I am. Even the leash is okay, because it tells me which way to go, instead of you just shouting all the time. But now you gave me this new fancy collar. More like a white funnel with my head at the bottom. Anyway, it's not working out.

It started last week. I was scratching my ear on account of the earache, which happened just after all the great swimming I did. It was around this same time that the whole side of my face got red—for no apparent reason.

That's when you gave me the big collar. You probably didn't realize it, but this keeps me from scratching myself, and every-thing itches more. The good news is I don't really mind the itch because the collar annoys me so much in so many ways.

I bump into things now. Doorways and furniture and trees. The inside of toilets. And when we go to play, the other dogs have all kinds of fun grabbing the collar and dragging me around the park. It's like a new game to them: "Axelrod with a Handle."

It's also hard to grab a stick or to play with Fetch. But I gotta say that catching a ball on the fly is a lot better. If I get within a foot or so, the ball just falls into the funnel and goes straight into my mouth.

I guess there are other good parts. The collar makes it more fun to drink water 'cause I can scoop it up from the bowl then carry it around with me for a while. And kids love me even more. They point at me and laugh. Then I wag my tail and go up to kiss them—and the collar knocks them sideways. Ha!

I may even miss this lovable thing when you finally take it off. You are going to take it off, aren't you? Because it's not lovable. And I'm not really going to miss it. I made that up.

AXELROD

My Home Remedy

I don't mind a flea. Gives me something to scratch, and it keeps my mind off of being a dog. The trouble is, a flea never stops with one. The next trouble is, Toby and his family don't notice, not at all, even when there's suddenly hundreds of them. I can be scratching and flailing all I want, but unless I'm flailing at a raccoon hiding up a hackberry tree, who cares?

That's why I came up with a home remedy, something that doesn't depend on Toby or anyone else. All on my own, I came up with this foolproof cure.

 The first step is to give yourself ticks. Sounds wild, but try it. The best place is the woods. Just lie down on some bushes or roll around in a dead bird. After a few ticks, I go back inside and nuzzle up to as many people as I can. Ticks are so much bigger that it's never long before someone (step two) kicks me out of the house and makes me sleep outside.

Step three is in the middle of the night when I ramble down the railroad tracks and keep an eye out for some wild dogs with mange. This can take hours. And then when you find one, you have to lie down next to it or play or have a fight. I know what you're thinking. Mange? It's ugly and painful. But hey, you already got fleas and ticks. What's a little mange?

Then you come home. That's step four. Time for a break.

For the next few days, I hang out, usu-ally outdoors since everyone knows I still have ticks and, of course, fleas, which was the whole point...except some-times I forget the point by this point since every spot on my entire body is itching like crazy.

Step five. I wander over to a neighbor's place. Step six. I howl and act miserable. That's pretty easy. Step seven is when the nice neighbor calls the sheriff and reports Toby for having a dog with fleas and ticks and the mange and maybe a few bruises from the wild dogs down by the tracks. It also helps to look skinny.

I guess steps eight through eleven are complicated, but not for me. The people at the shelter do it all and I get a few days away from home. The only bad part is that they yell at Toby for not taking care of me. But that's not totally bad.

So, that's my cure for fleas. If you don't like it, I do have another cure, but it's much more painful. I wouldn't recommend it.

Rufus T.

I Miss
Our Routine

I've been spending a lot of time at the vet lately, my days full of cages and short walks and vet food. You ever try vet food? It may be exactly the same as yours, but it doesn't taste like it. And they must put something weird in it, because half the time, I'm groggy. The only good part is I get plenty of time to think.

I think what I miss most when I'm at the vet, off the top of my head, is that you don't own a cage. The next thing I miss is the routine, the day-to-day stuff. Like coming home. No matter how bad my day. It doesn't matter how mean the cat was or what mood I'm in—the moment you walk through that door, you're happy. You wag your hands and talk in that voice and let me jump up. I can't tell you how nice it is having someone who always comes home, someone who loves me unconditionally, unlike the cat.

It's funny how much our daily routines matter. The way we both dance when you put down the food. Two shows a day and it never gets old. The way you always chase me around with a towel after we do the bath. The way you hide your favorite toy and make me go find it. Remember all the times you try to make the bed with me on it, and you throw me off and I get back on, and then you throw the sheets over my body and I run around? You may pretend to be mad at me, but you're not.

Okay, maybe these moments aren't special, but we've done them hundreds of times, so they are. They're the things I remember best. Not the big cow bone that took me a week to eat. Not all the lonely hours spent waiting by the door.

It's all the little, ordinary things, things we do over and over again, that make up a good life. That's what I think. And so I guess, when it's all said and done—and at some point it is all said and done—we've had a pretty good life.

Sophie

Canine Games

It may look like chaos, watching the seven of us run around like a pack of human toddlers...okay, that part is chaos. But we also play organized games—very organized, with very strict rules.

"PETTING TAG"

First—find a human. Then one dog puts himself under the human's hand and gets petted. This dog is called "it." Now all the other dogs try to get petted as well, squeezing in, whining, pawing, anything that works. They're also "it." That's the game. But it can go on for hours.

"THE BLAME GAME"

One dog secretly does something bad—peeing in undesignated areas, scratching furniture, recycling scraps from the open garbage. There's a long list, trust me. When the human starts yelling, all the dogs line up. The dog with the guiltiest expression on his face loses. Recently in our house it's been the puppy, which makes this everybody's favorite game by far.

"THE LAST BARK"

Simple, but a classic. One dog starts barking, probably for no reason. The others join in until the human starts yelling. The dogs keep barking and the human yells even more. The last dog to bark without actually getting punished wins.

"TOY MONOPOLY"

The dog who steals all the toys in the house wins. Like the human version, this can go on for weeks until no one cares anymore except the winner.

"TRIPPING"

This is less a game than a sport, and the playing field is usually the kitchen. The goal is to run around the human's ankles until he trips. If you yourself get injured, you're out. But if the human gets injured, you get a point and the honor of starting the next game. In good weather, tripping can be played outside with leashes, in which case it resembles tether ball. Tether ball with a human as the pole.

"THE SLEEPING MARATHON"

Kind of self-explanatory, except for the rules. Night-time sleeping doesn't count. Neither does drugged-out recovery time from an illness or injury. Neither does being a stuffed, mechanical animal with dead batteries. (Plushy had set a new household record of six days before we figured that one out.)

Charlie

Down, Dog, Down

Now that my boys are older, they stopped most of the bad stuff—the so-called bad stuff that you so-call bad. They finally got over biting hands and found that they don't like the pee smell in the house. They also limit their chewing to parts of the furniture you can't see. Any normal person would be thrilled. But not you. No. You have to come along and invent new bad things, things you used to think were cute.

I am referring, of course, to jumping up. I cannot count the number of times—in the millions maybe?—when Runt and Mutt Junior would come bounding up and throw their paws on your legs, and you loved it. You would coo like pigeons and pet their heads.

I guess the change came either just before or just after they knocked down the old person. Around that same time. But the woman didn't seem to mind. I remember clearly the words she said when you helped her up out of the gutter.

"No" and "problem," she said. No problem. Although I'm not sure she said them in the same sentence.

Jumping on people comes naturally, both to dogs and to people. We're not sure why you do it, but we do it because we like you and we're excited. It also gets us closer to making eye contact and much closer to your crotch. Need I say more?

But then you started giving them mixed signals, like shouting no and pushing them down. What does that mean? It could mean anything. Then a day later, you'd come home and they'd jump all over and you'd be fine. Even I got confused, and I don't really care.

A dog knows that there are two kinds of people—people who like us and people who don't. The people who like us don't mind the jumping, not at all. The people who don't like us also pretend not to mind, but you can tell. And then there are the people who wear white, who don't even pretend.

But the easiest way to get them to stop is to make them hate you. Is that what you want? You want them to run away when you come home? You want them to leave the room and cower in a corner by the hidden, chewed-up furniture leg? Is that why you got dogs in the first place?

I didn't think so.

Dimples

I Need My Jerky Treat

What are you guys doing in there? Hello? Hello? Please leave.

Technically, this is your guest cottage, I know. But I have a claim too. This is where you let your life coach live for a while. We became buddies, Edgar and me. He was cool. Every day, I walked over to the cottage and he would secretly give me a jerky treat from a box he kept under his bed. It was our little secret—and sometimes the only real meat I got all day.

Then he died, which seemed to be setting a bad example for a life coach. Everyone was sad—you, your friends, me—especially me since I knew there was still a whole bunch of individually wrapped jerkies under his bed.

The very saddest part was when you locked up the cottage. I must have worked for the next two days, looking for a way in. Finally one night I found a loose, rotted-out board behind the bathtub. With a little extra chewing, I managed to squeeze my body inside.

Right away, I saw a tiny light go on and off, which scared me until I remembered that the whole place was like this, with lights that keep blinking until you officially unlock the door. Anyway, the rest was pretty easy—crawling under the bed, lifting out exactly one jerky treat (no need to be selfish), and chomping it down, wrapper and all.

On that first night, I heard your voice outside the door. The blinking light must have scared you too. You were nervous. "Edgar? Edgar, is that you?" I didn't stop to think how odd that was, since Edgar was dead. I just scrambled back to the tub. By the time you unlocked the cottage door, I was standing on the grass by your feet, looking innocent, with just a hint of jerky on my breath.

Since then, I've been going in every night, taking just one piece and then sneaking out. And every night, you come by and unlock the door and call out Edgar's name. On the past couple of nights, you've been crying a little. That makes me sad, as sad as someone can be who just had a little taste of heaven.

But tonight is different. Tonight I can't crawl inside because you and a bunch of friends are already inside, sitting around his table, holding hands and staring into a crystal ball and saying, "Edgar, Edgar, talk to us."

I have no idea what you're doing. It's either way too smart for me or way too dumb. All I know is that I need you out of there so I can get my daily piece of beef.

☮ Moonbeam

I Want to Be You

I don't think about it much, only when I'm down. Like today. Today I found my first gray hair. Not even a year old; can you believe? And it wasn't growing somewhere harmless, like the middle of my face. No, I found it right under my tail, the first place another dog looks. It makes you wonder. What's it all about, this thing we call life? And why can't I be human? Is that too much to ask?

First off, I'm tired of short. Even for a dog, I'm short. Everything is a jump—beds, stairs, toilets. After a while—no offense—staring at your ankles loses its appeal. Humans are tall and have everything but tails. They can open cabinets and go outside on their own. They can explore dead things and no one bosses them around. Honestly, if I hear you scream "bad dog" one more time...

Oh, I know. You see me sleeping on the rug, not a care in the world—except for boredom and this burr under my ear and not knowing where my next meal is coming from, although it's probably that cabinet. You smile with envy and call this a "dog's life." Well, you should try it.

Ooh, what a great idea. Let's trade. You can do it. Anyone who can open the car door from across the street can certainly figure this out. Then you can be a tiny little dog trying not to get stepped on. All day you can follow me around, looking cute and turning some empty shampoo bottle into a toy.

Me, I'll be a human wearing delicious makeup and running off to all the exciting places. Do you ever go and do competitive eating, like we see on TV? I think I'd like that. Maybe hamburgers or chicken fingers. I can come home with a trophy and a teeny tiny doggie bag and make you beg and do tricks. At the end of the day, when we're both exhausted, then I'll hog all the space on the bed and say things like, "Hey, you get to sleep all day. Now it's my turn."

The next day, I promise to be there so we can switch back. I won't run away, I promise. We'll just switch back and everything will be normal again. I promise.

♡ Gabby

My Pack

Willow

NuNu

Flea

Bit

Tinkerbell

My Incredible Journey
By Tinkerbell

I am not a hero. Oh, my picture was in the papers and there have been tons of interviews. But I'm just an ordinary dog who happened to travel fifty miles and brave the wild elements in order to return to you, her beloved companion. That's all.

I wish I could tell you everything, darling, because the truth is probably even more harrowing than you imagine.

It began on that ferry ride back from Martha's Vineyard. It was a gorgeous day and we were out on the deck, you bundled in your furs and me in the Ferragamo tote by your feet. You had just gotten up to go yell at Brianna when the boat hit this big wave, totally out of nowhere. Even as I faced the prospect of death, I could see the horror on your face as the tote slid across the deck, took a hard bump against the rail, and tumbled into the deep cold sea.

I know you did everything to save me. I heard the alarm go off and saw the boat come to a slow, rocking stop in the water. Then someone pointed to what looked like a drowning rat desperately clinging to a floating marker. Everyone shouted. The ferry changed directions. But by the time you got to it, this drowning rat had slipped beneath the surface and disappeared.

It was nearly a week later when the miracle happened. You were just backing out of your driveway. And what did you see in your rearview mirror? Me. Bedraggled, dirty, and slowly limping home after what the news would soon call "the adventure of a lifetime."

I wouldn't quite call it that. True, there were horrendous moments. Like on the ferry, when I crawled out of your Ferragamo tote and into this man's beach bag because I thought I smelled a potato chip. The wave hit the boat just seconds later.

It was so traumatizing that I just stayed in his bag the whole way back. Didn't even raise my voice. Wait. It gets worse. Once they got home, he and his family just tossed the bag and me and all their beach stuff into the garage and shut the door.

It took me days and days to escape that garage, surviving on nothing more than leftover steak and half-eaten lobster. But when I finally did make it outside, I caught my first bit of luck. Their house was right across the road from your house. Everyone says how much I must love you to find my way home after such an ordeal. And they're right, of course. It's a very busy street, almost a highway.

As for the drowning rat, I can only assume that it was a real rat and it really did drown.

 Tails up

We're Not All That Great

You say it all the time. "Dogs are better than people." And you must believe it's true because I think you have more dogs than friends. Not including the mailman, I can count the number of visitors who come to the house on two paws.

I know you guys love us. We love you back—as much as we're able. But we're honestly no better than anyone. You've seen us fight over the same bone. Even humans don't do that. I'll bet we're as sneaky as you too. And most of us have this thing about squirrels, even though I guess some of them are nice and we shouldn't judge. By the way, have you ever killed a squirrel? Me neither. But it's not from lack of trying.

Maybe the reason you like us so much is that we follow you around and don't talk. If people did that, they'd be more likable. Plus, you don't expect too much of us. It's not like you're waiting for us to grow up and be more responsible and make a living. Or to come visit more often, because we're already there, so what's the point?

You're a lot more patient with us too. Like if the neighbor suddenly walked up to you and vomited, you might be annoyed. I bet you would. Yet when the neighbor's dog did that, you didn't get mad. You were worried. I don't mean to sound critical, but maybe your dog skills are better than your people skills.

Oh, and about loyalty? Being loyal and as faithful as a dog? Okay, we are loyal. I'll admit that. We have the loyalty thing down. For some reason it would be impossible for us not to wait by the door for you. Or to sit with you when you're sad. Or to follow you anywhere.

Maybe that does count for something. But it's not like we have any choice. You are our world. We depend on you. We can't imagine you not coming home and taking care of us, which brings up another point: we're not very imaginative.

But we are loyal.

Charlie

I LIFT ME UP

I don't mean to get all personal, but you seem endlessly fascinated by how I lift my leg. You watch all the time. You talk about it with strangers. You'll check to see if there's anything coming or if I'm shooting dry. Don't think I haven't noticed.

I remember back when I was a pup, the first time I propped up my leg on a tree. It was exciting. I was finally a big dog. It felt clean and natural, and you were so proud. "Look at my dog!" So I tried it next on a sofa.

Apparently, there are a ton of rules. No lifting indoors. No lifting my leg on your leg. No lifting on other people, unless they don't notice; then we just sneak away. Car tires are okay. Bike tires are not. Some bushes yes; some bushes no.

Of course, I like to lift where other dogs have gone before. But it's not a territory thing. Where'd you get that idea? I'm smart enough to know the hydrant isn't my territory. It's like a human signing a birthday card. That doesn't make it your card, just because you signed it. But it makes the card more personal. Same thing with pee.

One more thing. The higher I shoot, the better. Sometimes I'll try standing on my front paws, just to reach a little further up on the wall. I don't know why. Makes me feel good—kind of like when you stand taller or pull in your stomach when someone takes a picture. I mean, everyone knows you're short and sucking it in. But it makes you feel better. Same thing here.

It's not complicated. It's not like we demand a special room in the house where we have to pee into a cold, white chair full of water. Try explaining that one.

Although there were a couple times in the backyard, just you and me, when we both lifted our legs on the same tree. Nice. Like a bonding moment. And my pee landed a little higher up than yours. I'm just saying.

Bandana

I NEED A NEW JOB

An idea came to me today. You know, somewhere between getting up late and the first nap. By the time I settled into staring at the bathroom door, waiting for you to come out, I got to wondering. "Why do I have so much time to sit and wonder?" I wondered. "Am I retired? I think I'm retired."

I hope it's not true. But let's face it, you guys are treating me like chopped liver, delicious chopped liver that everyone loves. I'm not used to that. I'm used to working.

Sure, I still have my weekend job in the country. But even that doesn't seem like work anymore, especially since I make up my own chores and no one really cares. So I wind up following you around, staring at you or pawing at your leg. "Do you need me to walk you in the woods? Not right now? Do you need me to stay underneath your feet and trip you every time you turn? I can do that. See?"

I guess my trouble is I'm bored. What do you do when you're bored? I know you eat. I like eating too. You don't always share, but at least begging helps me deal with the boredom. Sometimes you talk to me—and I pretend to listen. Other times, you talk into a piece of plastic on your ear. But most of all, you sit on the sofa and play with another piece of plastic from the low table that smells like popcorn. I tried playing with the plastic, just like you. It worked great. All the sounds and the yelling and then chasing me around. But we can only play that game so many times. Then I'm bored again.

To be honest, I'm not sure I'm cut out for retirement. I like being useful, to get up every day with a purpose. I like people teaching me what to do and then expecting good things. And I don't like being treated like chopped liver, not unless I earn it. Then maybe as a reward, you could give me some real chopped liver. That would be nice.

SARGE

I SAVED YOUR LIVES

I knew the day would come. Too many kids walked up and pointed at my tummy and laughed. Too many puppies ran around me playing tag, like I'm a mountain. Too many bowls of ice cream disappeared. (For the record, I don't know how that happened. Why am I even mentioning it?)

So the diet wasn't a surprise. The treats stopped coming. Then the table scraps. Then the food level in my bowl went down. My first thought was to go on a hunger strike, but a few minutes later, I changed my mind.

What I decided to do was to beg more. Yes, I really can beg more, and I think I proved it. Begging during a walk, begging when I'm asleep, begging in the middle of dinner—my own dinner. I even tried separating the two of you and whining twice as much. Nothing happened but a sore throat, made even worse by the lack of any soothing ice cream.

I was just about to give up when I found out about the party. By the way, you guys make great party food, especially when you drop some or leave it on a low counter or let me taste.

But not this time. This time, you ignored me completely

and put the food straight into the refrigerator. That was wrong in so many ways, the main way being that you didn't give me any, not even your famous appetizer, guacamole dip.

After you left the kitchen, I scratched around the refrigerator, trying to get inside. When the door didn't open, I scratched on the side, thinking there must be an emergency side door. But I didn't get anywhere, except that the refrigerator rope came loose from the wall and it stopped making that sound.

It was hours and hours before the party started. When the people actually came, I went into my act again, jumping around the kitchen, trying everything I knew. Maybe that's why you didn't notice that the refrigerator was now kind of warm.

When you finally did bring out the appetizer, I was all over it. Guacamole, right in the middle of the coffee table. Yum, but kind of warm. You yelled at me and put me in the bedroom—until a minute later when I started throwing up. Then you took me to the vet, who said it was the spoiled guacamole and I was lucky to be alive.

Anyway, so I'm a hero. My brave actions saved all of your lives, if I'm not mistaken. And as a reward, you need to take me off this diet.

Orson

My Job Is Over

Time sure flies. It's been awhile since my boys were that kind of horrible, tear-your-hair-out trouble. You once thought the only answer might be to put down a dozen bags of kibble and move to a new country and not tell us. You miss those days, don't you?

Oh, don't deny it. We all miss the trouble. Getting out of bed each morning, not knowing exactly what you're stepping into, trying to figure out which puppy did what and how to stop it, arguing all evening about what went wrong and how to fix it and who's the worst parent.

I hear you reminiscing all the time. "Remember when Runt got into your closet and ate all your left shoes but not the rights?" (He loved your toe fungus, that's why.) Or "I still don't know how they managed to reach up to the outdoor grill and eat the steak." (That was a flock of pigeons. Honest. Or it could have been me.)

All of that is over, and the boys have turned into regular, boring dogs. They don't bounce anymore; they walk. Their bodies are bigger and their heads look smaller, which is not so cute. It's like nature's way of telling you to stop saying, "Sweeeet!"

There's a reason why dogs start out as cute puppies. It's to help you survive all the trouble. Now there are no more little naps on top of the whirring dryer. No more puke in those right-foot shoes that you can't use anymore anyway. No more hikes around the neighborhood, shouting their names until you're hoarse because someone snuck into the garbage can and got accidentally put out on the curb.

What do you have to talk about now? Your kids? Sure, but that's too serious. Your own lives? You can try having a conversation about your own lives, but it's going to be boring.

I guess the only solution is to get more puppies—not that I'm volunteering. My puppy days are over. But there are always more puppies in the world. And your furniture is already a mess and the house will always smell of urine, always. So you have nothing to lose. It'll be a ton of fun and trouble, just what you need.

And remember...I'll always be here with that good advice.

Dimples

THE END

Our Special Place

On most days, you and me take a ride in the car. We walk into a building where the doors open by magic. Then a moving closet take us up to the place you call "work." Inside your room is a dog bed and water bowl just for me. But most of my day I spend walking around, getting petted and asking for food, while you sit there talking to other people or thin air, or looking at the box on your desk.

One of the first things I do every day is empty wastebaskets. Just the ones with food wrappers. Food wrappers are what we like to call recyclable, which is just a fancy word for "I eat them." Sometimes when I "recycle" too much, then my tummy has to "recycle" everything again, either on the rug or under your desk. Then you "recycle" it into another wastebasket. Then I find that wastebasket and we start over.

The moving closet is also loads of fun. I can sneak right on, if there's a bunch of people paying no attention. We wind up in a work place just like yours but different. Or we wind up outside where I just go and sit by your car until you come find me. Or your friends and me go up on the roof where they throw away cigarette butts and I retrieve them. Then I "recycle" them.

In the middle of the day, you and me go for a walk. But I can also go walk anytime I want. I really can. You see, one day I found this magic hook on the wall by your room. All I have to do is pull the hook. It's very small, not made for a dog. But when I pull it down, there's a noise. Very loud and long. You and your friends hear it and come out of your rooms and look around. And then everybody takes me outside for a walk and we watch all the long trucks that come and park out front.

Sometimes I think you get bored—like when you shut your door and take a nap. But you shouldn't get bored. I can always find fun things. There's a button inside the moving closet that makes it stop. Did you know that? There's also food on a shelf beside the cold-box. And you haven't lived until you tromped all around the place with coffee grounds on your feet. C'mon.

Work is fun.

AXELROD

My Purpose

Let's be honest. I talk a good game, but I'm probably never going to run away and be a dancer. I'll probably never see Maggie again or be as popular as Burnside. But at least I have a purpose. Every dog needs a purpose. And mine is taking care of Toby.

Look at me right this second. Toby and his pals put me smack in the middle of Hill Road, guarding them so they can go sledding. The cars all stop and honk their horns at the big dumb dog. Then they give up and take the dirt road instead. If it wasn't for me, you see, Toby might get run over. But I'm helping, just like a big stone or a log blocking the top of the road, watching them playing and laughing without me and...okay, I suppose my job could be done by a big stone or a log. Dang! Now I'm depressed.

I remember back when Toby couldn't get enough of me. My eyes were barely open and there he was, always petting me, sneaking me to school in his lunch box. Then we was hunting buddies, every day from the week before hunting season to two weeks after. So when did we stop being bestest friends? I don't know. 'Cause now I'm lying spread-eagle on a patch of black ice, staring down a tanker truck and feeling dumb.

Maybe I need to rethink my purpose. I'm still young. I can howl for hours. I can keep a thousand smells straight in my head, even "new car," which I only smelled once a long time ago. There must be something I can do. Maybe with perfumes. If I run away, and this time for good...

Oh, here comes Toby walking up the hill, tired from having so much fun. I wonder what he wants me to do now? Pull the sled home? Eat his homework? Be a running target so he can practice throwing snowballs?

Don't try petting me, Toby. It's not going to work. (Ooh, behind the ears! I love behind the ears.) And don't try giving me that treat from your pocket. (Ooh, liver. I love liver.) And don't try calling my name and throwing a stick. (Look, Toby, I can fetch with my eyes shut, just from your smell on the stick. Aren't I a good boy?)

Sorry. What was I saying? Something about purpose?

Rufus T.

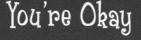

You're Okay

We've been together awhile and it's not so bad anymore. I can barely remember what happened before you took me in. Something about water? I'm asking because every time you put me in the bath, I have this urge to climb up on a roof.

We're into the habits of our life, and I'm the kind of girl (a dog) who likes regular habits. By now I'm used to the flowery smell on your hands. I don't mind the prayer flags flapping all over the dog house. Ditto the afternoon meditation, except when you wake me with your snoring. The vegan diet is annoying, but if I pretend I just tracked down and killed the soy, it's fine.

Dogs can get used to anything. The music that never begins or ends but just plays all day. The plastic, hard-to-eat flowers on the shrine. And at first I thought the prayer wheel was a crappy toy, but now I learned how to spin it with my tail.

After you stopped taking me along to your so-called silent retreats every month, I even got used to staying at the new-age kennel. They let us decide our own meal times there. (I choose "constant.") And ever since they started keeping the dogs and cats in the same play area, everyone gets a ton of exercise, especially the cats.

That reminds me...one of the dogs at the kennel said you and me are starting to look alike. Isn't that funny? And so far from the truth. True, I wear a rainbow collar and you wear a rainbow dress. And you have this careful way of walking because you don't want to step on any ants. I don't like stepping on them either, but just because they squish and crunch and get between my toes. So maybe we do look kind of similar when we walk. But not really. For one thing, your aura is kind of bluish-green and my aura is more brownish and...

Wait a minute. I don't have an aura. Auras don't exist. This is all just silliness and we're not anything at all alike. Forget I even brought it up.

☮ Moonbeam

My Pack

Willow

NuNu

Flea

Bit

Tinkerbell

Don't Ever Leave Me
By Tinkerbell

The open suitcase, the smell of spray tan, the week-long binges on rice cakes and cottage cheese…it took me a few times to figure it out, but I'm not an idiot. Brianna's staying with her dad, and you're going on a trip.

I probably shouldn't take it so hard, but no one spoils me when you're gone, especially not Consuela, who doesn't have a nice purse to give me rides in and who treats me, I hesitate to say, almost like a dog.

Now, I'm not by nature a manipulative creature. I'm not. You believe me, right? Well, that just proves how good I am.

Remember that one week, when you kept saying, "Ariba, ariba, ariba," to all your friends? Or it could have been "Aruba." I waited until I saw you put your pill cases in the suitcase, then I went out to the garden and got burrs stuck in all four of my paws. Sure it hurt. But I limped around like a broken windup toy, and by the time we got out of the doctor's office, you had decided to stay home and nurse me back to health.

The next time was easier. On the morning when you put out your pills, I simply chewed through the plastic and swallowed a few. I felt really weird—very relaxed and nervous at the same time. On the up side, I think it got rid of that cold sore on my lip. Anyway, another tragedy averted. But you were starting to get suspicious, and that wasn't good.

Then the warning signs started again. I did everything I could to stop you from going. I chewed through your bathing suit and your new collection of Spanx. You went out and bought more. I whined constantly and gnawed my fingernails, but apparently you don't consider that unusual behavior. As the trip drew closer, you were looking pretty smug. So I really had no choice.

This morning, I went out to the part of the yard where the gardener never goes. They have this shiny ivy there. It doesn't do a thing for me personally, but I know how you people react. I rolled around in the ivy for a while. Then I came over to you on the patio and kissed you. We played and played, just like old times, and it made you giggle and smile.

This time you came very close to driving away. But then the bumps on your skin showed up and you started crying and everything worked out for the best.

Is it my fault I love you so much that I never want you to leave?

Tails up

What's Wrong With Me?

I'm not quite sure what's happening. It all started around the time of my twelfth birthday party—the big one in April, not the small one in March. That's when you changed my food without even asking. And, unless I'm mistaken, you're using the word "dog" a lot more. May I suggest going back to "puppy"? I like "puppy."

There are other things that are changing too. Toys aren't as much fun, especially after I decided they're not real. I can share food and force myself to drink out of someone else's bowl. And I'm becoming vaguely aware that other things exist besides me. This is annoying.

Like when we walk by infant puppies on the street. It wasn't long ago when I could compete with the best of them. I would roll on my back and go floppy and pretend the grass was my enemy. With a little effort, I could make you say "ahh" just as much as a three-month-old. Now I don't even want to. In fact, I'm saying "ahh" just like you, in my own way. Aren't infant puppies precious? They are so cute. I want one of my own. No, I want several. Can you buy me some puppies of my own?

Augh! See? That's what I'm talking about.

And it's not just my feelings that are mixed up. It's my body. I'm a lot more tender underneath. I'm putting on weight. And I throw up in the morning. That's not weird. But I don't feel like eating it afterward, even though it's smelly and gooey and warm. And that is weird.

I was talking about this the other day with Sam. He's the long-haired dachshund I had sex with. He says what I'm going through is perfectly normal, but I'm not sure. Is it normal to start hearing a whole bunch of heartbeats coming from inside you? Something must be wrong with my heart.

I just want things back to normal. I want to stay small and helpless and be the center of everyone's world. I want to stay a puppy. Aren't puppies cute? Don't you just want to hug them and protect them and think about them all the time?

♡ Gabby

I'm Not Irreplaceable

This is probably the last thing you want to hear right now. But you'll get another dog. At least you should. And you'll love it just as much. Because the truth of the matter is that I'm unique and irreplaceable, like you keep saying...but I'm not.

This is the biggest dog secret of all. Every single one of us is unique, no matter how ordinary. You think back to those times when I was a puppy and followed you into the field of snow and jumped from one deep footprint into the next, trying to catch up. Or that time you hung up the bug zapper on the porch and couldn't for the longest time figure out why I kept crawling under the house. And all those snuggly evenings on the couch, just sitting there petting each other. Do you really think no other dog could do that?

Maybe I'm unique because I'm part of these memories you'll